LOVE
Bytes

LOVE
Bytes

Romance – Family – Friendship – Humanity

KAREN McMILLAN

Powerfresh Ltd

Dedication

For Stephen

First published in the UK in 2006
by Powerfresh Ltd
Unit 3, Everdon Park
Heartlands, Daventry
NN11 8YJ

First published by
Random House New Zealand
18 Poland Road, Glenfield, Auckland, New Zealand
www.randomhouse.co.nz

ISBN 1 90496 731 0

Photographs: Christine Hansen
Cover and text design: Christine Hansen
Printed in China

Contents

Love

Love is all we have, the
only way that each can help
the other.

Euripides

I may have all knowledge and understand all secrets; I may have all the faith needed to move mountains — but if I have no love, I am nothing.

I Corinthians 13: 2

Love is all around, everywhere you look. It is in the warm breath of a smiling grandmother with her granddaughter nestled in her arms. It is in the exuberant faces of brother and sister racing each other into the surf on a languid day at the beach. It is in the tender embrace of a young couple beginning on their married journey together through the labyrinth of life. It is there among the extended family gathered on the marae to farewell one of their own. And it is in the selfless, caring hand extended to another in need. Love is what binds us together. It is the glue for human relationships. For a ragged humanity it is our best trait, the only trait worth cultivating. In a world with poverty, hunger, war and terrorism, love is the only answer. Love is the antidote to hate. Kindness is the remedy for aggression. Compassion and caring are the solution to suffering. Forgiveness is the way forward when there are wrongs.

The word 'love' can be confusing, however. We can say, 'I love ice cream', and in the next breath say, 'I love you, Mum.' We love nature: sunsets, picturesque landscapes and vibrant wildlife. We love activities: skiing, surfing, hunting. Advertising executives urge us to love our possessions, our houses, our cars, our mobile phones. We most certainly love people: our parents, our children, our lovers, our friends. 'Love' is an umbrella word in English with many different facets. Aroha, alofa, 'ofa, sarang – the different languages of the world offer many other words that provide subtle, varying interpretations of love also.

Love Bytes explores the four types of love that exist between people using the Greek words for love – Eros: romantic, passionate love; Storgé: family love; Philia: the love between friends; and Agápe: the God-like love of all humanity.

In every community throughout the world you can witness examples of these different loves. Couples are kissing for the first time; others are celebrating their golden wedding anniversary. Newborn babies are adding joy to households; while in other homes families are coming together to help each other cope with the death of a loved one. Friends stand side by side on sports' fields, in churches and in movie queues. And countless compassionate people are helping our old, our disabled, those who are hurting and unsure.

Love is active rather than passive. How people express love to each other varies. For some, love is affirming words that encourage other people and make them feel loved. Other people do kind deeds that are practical, like painting the fence or fixing a bike. Some show love with physical closeness. Others enjoy quality time, simply hanging out together and taking the time to listen. And then there are those who like to give small, thoughtful gifts.

We need to use our understanding of the person we love when we show our love to them, however. We need to be aware of their preferences rather than projecting onto them simply what we would want. There is no point bringing home a rose for your wife every night if she thinks they are a waste of money, and if she simply longs to sit down and enjoy your company uninterrupted for twenty minutes instead. Likewise there is no point throwing a big surprise party for someone who doesn't like big gatherings and would prefer an intimate dinner with only a handful of friends. We all have different upbringings, personalities and natural preferences, so learning how to best show love to another person can sometimes take some thought. But with genuine love as our motivation there is always a way to show someone, successfully and lovingly, that we care.

Love is the most important aspect of our lives. Without love our lives are empty shells. Without love we merely exist. With love we are able to become vibrant, passionate and caring people living fully. So as we live our lives, let's take every opportunity to love others well.

Love meanings

Three syllables give the Maori word 'aroha' the drop on the English word 'love'. This is why I have always preferred to make love in Maori; you've got more romance to play with. Of course I am saying all this with a twinkle in my eyes, but 'aroha' really does have more resonance. It doesn't just encompass passionate love or romantic love but also sympathetic love, communal love, or even love for the world we live in. It's the kind of emotion that stirs us and makes us feel pure joy.

Witi Ihimaera

What does the word *love* mean to different people? Responses vary, but whatever people's background and native language one thing is clear: love is a verb. Love – the feeling – is a consequence of this verb. To love is to take action.

The word *love* means so many things; there are so many types of love. There is the love I have for my husband – passionate and trusting. There is the love I have for my children – nurturing. And then there is the love I have for friends – respect and caring.

Sara, 40s

The most beautiful language in the world to listen to is Samoan. And the word for love, *alofa*, stirs the spirit to acts of kindness, generosity and compassion. That is what *alofa* is all about.

Siosiua, 32

The Tongan word for love is *ofa*. It conveys a meaning of reciprocal love and sharing.

Aritelu, 27

In Korean *ae-jung* is affection, while *sarang* is love. But I think *ae-jung* is more important. It takes time to develop and is the foundation for *sarang*. Love is weak without affection.

Kyung-Soon, 41

The word for love in Chinese has a meaning that is more modest than in Western culture. For example parents are unlikely to say 'I love you' but they will do kind things and give their children gifts. Parents serve their children and in that way they show they love them. Living in New Zealand I see other approaches to the Chinese way.

Athena, 20s

The word *love* to me means an open-hearted, unconditional acceptance of another person. There are varying degrees of love, but it starts and ends with accepting that person for who they are, warts and all. The Japanese word for love is *ai* and it means the same in Japanese as it does in English, although the Japanese aren't terribly demonstrative – my aunts and uncles always get a bit of a shock when I give them a big hug!

Sonia, 30s

It has always seemed to me that *love* is a word that has been dealt to badly by the type of shift in meaning that is so common in a living language, and that the meaning of the word has probably been trivialised by overuse and abuse by generations of soft-focussed weepy movies and women's magazines. To be sure, romance is often an element of love, but it ain't all of love. And the way *love* is thrown about in writing and in speech nowadays, it seems to have become degraded to a status that's too lowly to cover the territory it needs to. Love should encompass sacrifice, sharing, forbearance, patience, charity, forgiveness, understanding, tenderness, romance, toughness, resilience, courage, giving, taking, reward, cost, obligation and consequence. Heavy stuff for one little word.

So we need another word. And aren't we lucky we live in New Zealand: we can absorb another word into our English – *aroha*. To me *aroha* is still a word that is big enough to cover all the territory. It is a word that belongs to a culture where reciprocity is normal in all facets of life, so it is clear that the feelings expressed should be reciprocated. If you gave love, you expected it to be returned. So *aroha* will do me nicely for the appropriate word, thank you.

Bruce, 50s

Aroha calls to the deepest part of who you are. *Aroha* sees your insecurities and imperfections and welcomes you regardless. *Aroha* has arms that reach across a void and carry us home to a place of security and acceptance. *Aroha* spurs us on to great and mighty deeds and stirs our faith into action. *Aroha* brings healing to brokenness.

Tracey, early 40s

Eros

ROMANTIC LOVE

How do I love thee? Let me count the ways.

I love thee to the depth and breadth and height

My soul can reach, when feeling out of sight

For the ends of Being and ideal Grace.

Elizabeth Barrett Browning

Eros is the Greek word for romantic, passionate, sexual love. In Greek mythology, Eros was the god in charge of physical love. And through the ages history and literature have romanticised many passionate lovers. There is the tortured love of Heathcliff and Cathy in *Wuthering Heights*. There are the doomed romances of Romeo and Juliet; Anthony and Cleopatra; Lancelot and Guinevere – even Bonnie and Clyde. But still people cling to the story of Cinderella and Prince Charming who lived happily ever after. At Prince Charles and Lady Diana Spencer's 'fairytale' wedding we wanted and expected them to have a long and happy marriage. Despite the poor chances of success many couples do find true love, however. Poets Robert and Elizabeth Barrett Browning enjoyed many happy years of marriage. Scientists Marie and Pierre Curie loved and worked side by side in harmony. Shah Jahan built the Taj Mahal in memory of his beloved wife Arjumand Banu.

In Maori mythology, Tutanekai and the beautiful Hinemoa were in love. Nightly, on Mokoia Island, Tutanekai played flutes that Hinemoa could hear across the water in Owhata, four kilometres away. But her people were suspicious and every evening dragged their waka up to prevent her from paddling across to Mokoia Island. One night she made up her mind to swim across Lake Rotorua to meet with Tutanekai. They slept together – which signified marriage – and in the morning, instead of the expected war between their two peoples, there was peace and much rejoicing.

Romantic love is exhilarating and euphoric, but it is after the first flush of new romance and summer passion – when couples experience an autumn season of doubt – that they have the opportunity to build a more genuine, mature love. After the moonlight comes the hard work. And it is because we are emotional people at our cores that intimate relationships are both important to nurture and worth the extra effort if love loses any gloss. Because of real love, couples choose to nurture each other's growth. Couples accept and appreciate the quirks in each other's personalities. They learn that no relationship is perfect but they are still able to build a loving and strong union together. Each can choose to love the other, through good times and bad, with compassion, commitment and loyalty.

True Eros is not dumb or blind. It is not passive. It is a love that is active and fully aware: to have a successful intimate relationship, it has to be. People bring different backgrounds, experiences and emotional baggage to this special relationship. In Eros two people do not become one: instead two become three. As well as being 'you' and 'I', couples create an 'us' that was never in existence before. That is the magic and the power of Eros.

Looking for love

Tall, dark and averagely handsome, 42-year-old man from the
Waikato seeks woman with view to a long-term relationship.
Sincere and easy-going with a great sense of humour, I enjoy
outdoor sports, walks on the beach and moonlight dinners.
Is my soul mate out there?

Advertisement on New Zealand dating website

It is no wonder that so many people are looking for love, for that special person they can share their lives with. Being in a loving relationship is a privilege. It means you have gained someone who will have your best interests at heart, someone with whom you can be more of yourself than you have ever dreamed. It is a powerful mystery when two people meet, fall in love and then move from romance to true love. The quest is noble, success unsure, but the reward can be a vibrant, emotional union that lasts a lifetime.

Romance is like jellyfish: my worst fear!

Miller, 10, who has a phobia of jellyfish

In movies people always fall in love with each other because they are beautiful but in real life people aren't always beautiful. People fall in love with each other's personalities.

Jaimie, 10

I was separated and I'd had a few other girlfriends in the meantime. I didn't know what I wanted but I knew what I didn't want. I met Sarah at a barbecue. She was just so easy to talk to and good-looking. I'm not a romantic. I don't believe in love at first sight and that sort of stuff, but I just knew she was the one. I told my friends the next day that I had met the girl I was going to marry. Some of my friends knew Sarah and they just laughed. 'She's too good for you, mate.' We've now been married for nine years.

Richard, 42

I was living with a guy for over four years but then our relationship drifted apart. He was away a lot on business and he fell in love with someone else. That was difficult. I spent an entire year not going out with anybody before I decided I was ready to have another relationship. I am 48 and I don't want to be by myself. I want a partner in life who lives with me and is someone I can share everything with. I want someone who thinks like me, who is positive and who is an achiever. Someone who is caring and who makes me feel good about myself.

So I began actively seeking love. I joined a dating agency but that didn't work for me. I was introduced to five men. Each time I was rung up by the agency and told the man's name and what they did for a living and that was all I knew. Then the man would phone and we would arrange to meet for coffee and see how it went. One guy I went out with briefly but then decided he wasn't for me. His idea of a relationship and my idea of a relationship were just poles apart. He thought it was fine if he saw me once a week. And that is not what I was after.

So then I tried the internet approach because you never meet anyone nice in pubs. You just don't. The site I joined has five pages of profile on each person including a photo. Everyone is on a level footing. It is a fantastic site and I met five men through this website. One of the guys I thought was really nice but he ended up being just a dance partner. We went out dancing five nights a week, but then I realised that we never talked and there was nothing else to the relationship. But a few months ago I met a wonderful man through the website – and this is it. I've found the man I was seeking. He has blown me away. We both have the same determination and goal-setting. We talk for hours and hours and spend a lot of quality time together. He is wonderful!

Roxanne, 48

The first meeting

Love at first sight is easy to understand. It's when two people have been looking at each other for years that it becomes a miracle.

Sam Levenson

Ask any happy couple how they met and they will have no problem talking about the moment they first rested eyes on each other. Whether they were instantly attracted to each other, or even disliked each other initally, or simply thought they had found a lovely new friend, this moment in time remains a special memory to be treasured in the framework of their relationship.

We met each other when we were teenagers at the pictures – and now we have been married for 41 years. I can still remember our first gentle kiss! The thing I love most about Peter is that he is simply being who he is. He is trustworthy, mellowed, true blue, sexy, deep – not a talker, but he opens up when he chooses to. And I love it that back then he pointed out to his mother that I was the girl he was going to marry! The love we have now is as perfect and secure as anyone could ever ask for.

Diana, 50s

I met my future husband at my parents' home. I was visiting them and was out shopping with my mother when she said, 'We had better get home. Your dad has asked a young chap around from work.' 'Not another clod-hopper!' I said, and yes, this was the man I was married to for more than 61 years!

Jean, 86

I met my husband through a mutual friend's dinner party. My first impressions of him were that he was cute and a very gentle person. We got together as a couple a few months later. I was only fourteen at the time. We have now known each other for twenty years. We are best friends and have a happy marriage. I love his devotion to his family and his good heart.

Mandy, 30s

PENNY: We met on a blind date. I was doing a friend a favour as she didn't want to go.

DAVE: When we first met I just knew she was the one. Although it was very rocky to begin with. On the second date I took her to a wine and cheese party and she went home with somebody else. It was terrible!

PENNY: I finished with Dave, and went out with another guy for a while. Then six months later there was a knock at the door and Dave turned up. My mum said, 'Why don't you just get to know him?'

DAVE: We have been together ever since.

Dave and Penny, married for more than 30 years

I met Jean in the boozer, after work, while doing a course after coming back from Singapore. Started chatting up this bespectacled WRAC and discovered in the process she was changing her trade from general clerical to librarian. I am a bookworm. BINGO! The relationship we have now is like the Cold War. It is MAD (Mutually Assured Destruction) so each of us has to take great care not to push the button that launches the first strike, and no-one dare blink just in case that's when it happens. I would describe our love as a work in progress and the thing I love most about Jean is that she tolerates me.

Bruce, married for 'two-and-a-half life sentences, at today's going rate'

We were both working on a movie in Queenstown. I arrived on set for lunch and I saw him walking in the opposite direction: it was a 'slow motion' moment, love (or lust) at first sight. We chatted over lunch, then one night I met him by chance at a bar. We found we had a lot in common and on the spur of the moment I asked him to go to Wanaka with me for the weekend. We met up on the Saturday morning, rented a car and drove to Wanaka. It could have ended up platonic but it didn't! We've been together ever since. I didn't really believe something like this could happen!

Kat, 31, recently married

We met through mutual friends at a football match. He had been concussed and I was sent to offer him a cup of tea. We have now known each other for 50 years.

My husband was recently diagnosed with terminal cancer. When we had the result of the last scan we came home that night and cried together, holding each other through a sleepless night. Now we treat each day as a bonus.

I feel spiritual values have helped our marriage. We made our vows before God and He has always been part of our marriage. We've certainly had our arguments but we have always resolved them. We have five children, six grandchildren, not a lot of money, but we love each other more now than ever.

Jean, 68

A modern love story

Something so strong
could carry us away

Neil Finn

Sallie shares her story of finding love on the internet.

Lee and I first met online through ICQ. This is a search engine and it is a great way to connect up with people from all over the world with similar interests. Neither Lee nor I were looking for a relationship. I just wanted someone to talk to. Lee was online talking to a friend when I sent him a message. He said that he usually did not answer messages when talking to someone else but that night he felt compelled to. I am glad he did as we are now married!

I decided to meet Lee in person because he is very genuine and we got on so well. I had talked to a lot of people online and you can tell when you hit it off with someone. We both had the same sense of humour and we made each other laugh a lot. The way we thought about life was in line with each other. We both had the same attitudes to children (we both have three) and we generally felt for each other. We chatted online and on the phone for three months and decided it was worth the risk to meet. Lee was unable to leave his job at the time so I flew to the UK to meet him as I also had family there to stay with.

My first impressions of Lee were wonderful. He was just as he had described himself. We had both been totally honest about what we looked like so there were no surprises. Neither of us is as young as we were. Neither of us are bad-looking but we are not 20 either. One nice thing was that Lee's voice in real life just made me want to melt away! We were very sensible about our meeting too. We had in place safety nets in case we didn't hit it off in real time, but they were not needed.

Lee proposed to me on the phone two months after we had first met. He proposed again three days later when we met face to face in the UK. He was on bended knee. It was very romantic, on a windswept hilltop overlooking a beautiful bay on the west coast of England. We married in New Zealand. It was a lovely ceremony, held outside under an oak tree in a beautiful park .

The thing I most love about Lee is the way he talks to me. All the time! We hardly ever watch TV; most of the time we talk and have the most incredible conversations about anything and everything. The love we have together is very powerful and intense. We have made a total commitment to each other and we both intend to make this relationship work.

Lee tells me every day that he loves me. He has made me feel good about myself and about my body. He never puts me down and he is always positive and loving. Almost the first thing he said to me was, 'What's not to love, Sallie?' I was worried as I was a little overweight but Lee has displaced any fears I had. He is a very good person and is much liked by everyone who meets him.

He is also very kind. He cooks when I am tired or ill. He will do all the housework at those times without being asked! He makes all the tea and coffee when we are together. He buys me a rose on every special date. Unless Lee is at work, we spend all our time together. We visit friends, sightsee, talk a lot and watch movies cuddled up. We are always in close contact.

Sallie, 40s

Love after a long wait

I confess that I love him, I rejoice that I love him, I thank the maker of Heaven and Earth that gave him to me. The exultation floods me.

Attributed to Emily Dickinson

After 44 years of living with and caring for her parents, Joy shares how she met her husband and talks about the beautiful, loving relationship they now enjoy.

I lived with my parents until they died. They had me when they were older in life: I arrived on my mother's 40th birthday. I had a brother who was 11 years older than me and he departed from the house when he married at age 26. And everyone waited and waited for me to find someone – but I never did. My father died at the age of 86 and my mother 13 months later. They had been married for 57 years. I felt really comfortable still living with them and caring for them as they got older and had spent some time over the last few years preparing myself for the time when I would be on my own. However, no matter how much you prepare yourself for grief you don't know what it is like until it happens. I was 44 when my mother died.

About six months after Mum died I met Chris. Someone we both knew through our jobs introduced us. She was talking to Chris one day and he was saying how hard it was to find someone to meet. He had never married either and is 10 days younger than me. My face popped into her mind and she told Chris about me.

She asked if I wanted to meet Chris and told me about him. I said yes. I wouldn't normally have met someone on a blind date – I am a more cautious person than that. But a week or so before this I had been having a heart-to-heart with God telling Him that if there was someone out there for me it was the right time now. So Chris and I met. And we talked until two the next morning. We had so much in common it was amazing. We found out we were born in exactly the same place in Wellington; our mothers died nine days apart; we both liked art: Chris is an art teacher and I paint. On our second date we went sketching together.

Four months later we were in love – and eight months after we met we married. We have known each other for nine years now.

Our relationship is extremely close. Almost immediately after we married we developed a bond that couples usually take years to have. We can finish each other's sentences. We are often thinking of the same thing and will start to talk about it at the same time. We have never had an argument as neither of us likes conflict, so we agree to disagree or work out a compromise. I was diagnosed with breast cancer three years ago. Everything seems okay now but the chemo has affected me sexually. Chris doesn't mind. He wants to cuddle me each night when we go to bed and shows a lot of affection by holding and stroking me. I think I am the most fortunate person.

What I most love about Chris is his thoughtfulness and caring, even over small things, like where we go at the weekend. He always consults me about things and we make decisions together. And the care and support he has given me during my breast cancer experience – and the way he deals with how it has affected our sex life – demonstrates the strength of his love for me.

I certainly would not want to be without my beloved Christopher and wouldn't have missed this experience of love and marriage for anything!

Joy, 50s

Wedded bliss

The great love I have hitherto expressed to you
Is false, and I find my indifference towards you
Increases daily. The more I see of you the more
You appear in my eyes an object of contempt
I feel myself in every way disposed and determined
To hate you. Believe, I never had any intention
To offer you my hand ...

Amelia Webb, in a coded letter to Nicholas Loye

Amelia Webb was instructed by her parents to cease communications with her beloved Nicholas. Dutifully she wrote a letter breaking it off with him and showed it to her parents. But she added a postscript before sealing the envelope. 'After reading this please read it again, missing every second line.' Three months later Amelia and Nicholas married and they emigrated to New Zealand in 1862.

Getting married is like a tandem parachute jump. There may be bad weather or aircraft trouble that prevents you from getting off the ground. There is a danger you will be hurt. But for those who have found the right partner and who are committed to the journey, it can be the beginning of the most exhilarating and wonderful experience of life. And a wedding is the start of creating something larger than yourself: a marriage.

I reckon you should get married. It is a tradition for people – but you have to be really careful to choose the right person. My mum and my dad separated.

Lizzie, 10

We got married at the end of last year. We went to the 'Burning Man' festival in the Nevada Desert with 30,000 other people. We got married in front of 20 friends we met while at the festival. In the middle of the ceremony there was a white-out dust storm. Michael and I were alone, holding hands and closing our eyes against the fine alkaline dust. Then the elements released us, the wind and the dust subsided and we were married. We had a wedding that was great for us in an environment that we loved, plus we had an amazing day with friends and family in New Zealand later. We both know that each other is 'the one'. The only thing we wish for is more fun times together.

Kat, 31

Graeme and I met on a blind date 13 years ago when my son Marvin was four. Our wedding day was very special. Graeme, Marvin and I swapped rings: it symbolised the three of us committing to each other. What I most love about them is they love me unconditionally, they are great fun to be with and they challenge me to be a better person. I am very blessed to have two such special men in my life!

Josie, 40

On our first date Noel took me to a 21st birthday party. It was coming up to my own 21st and Noel rang me a few days later. He asked me what I would like for my birthday. I said I didn't know. He said, 'What about a diamond ring?!' I had been planning to go to England but I didn't do that; instead we announced our engagement at my 21st birthday, which was nine days after our first date. We got married at the Holy Trinity Church and that was 46 years ago. We just knew it was right.

Earline, 60s

I think every bride gets a little stressed out in the lead-up to the wedding day. You want everyone to be happy but also to be happy yourself. But it was fine on the day. I've always wanted to get married in the islands so that is what we did. I got on a little canoe with this warrior guy and my dad. Everyone was on the small island across from the main one and drums were beating and we made our way across the water to them. We got married on the beach and it was everything I could have wanted. I love everything about my husband, he is amazing – and our wedding day was hot but very relaxed and lovely.

Sonia, early 30s

I wouldn't mind getting married one day but I worry about the guns. In films there are men fighting over a woman and someone always gets shot.

How-Shin, 9

How come you have to wear a wedding dress? That's the only thing stopping me.

Esther, 10

From Serbia to New Zealand with love

Oh, my love, my love.
We form a single shadow.
We are hand in glove.

Iain Sharp

A Serbian couple who migrated to New Zealand share their beautiful and dramatic story of love.

DRAGANA: Zoran and I have our 10th wedding anniversary this Saturday. We met 12 years ago in Belgrade. I graduated from university with a degree in molecular biology, but wasn't sure what I wanted to do next so I had a three-month temp job. I was sitting at reception in the window when he came in wanting to send prune juice to some place I had never heard of. Then we ran into each other in the elevator, just by accident. We got talking and I told him I was taking a job at the university. He asked me out for a drink to celebrate and then he asked me out to dinner and that is how it all started.

ZORAN: Absolutely incorrect! One day on my way to the office I saw a sad beautiful girl sitting in the reception window. I was hoping to get her out of her sadness and out of the window, because my life would be fine then.

I found an excuse to go into that office, to approach her and everything is history.

DRAGANA: Zoran looked then as he is today. He is an eternal optimist and is always smiling. When we met he was just back from Cyprus and he was suntanned, relaxed and good-looking. That was him and still is!

ZORAN: We had had very different lives. I lived in a different part of the city and I had been a professional dancer for 10 years. I'd had a beautiful life touring the world. Then I had been working for a couple of years for a corporate company when I met Dragana.

DRAGANA: I'd never known anyone who had been a professional dancer. These were traditional Yugoslav dances. When we met it was an unsettled time as it was the beginning of the end of the former Yugoslavia. We had had more than 40 years of peace and our country was comparable to New Zealand in terms of security. It was a very peaceful country with a nice lifestyle. No one knew what was going to happen. After all, this was the middle of Europe, it was the end of the 20th century and the only thing we had heard about war was half a century ago.

ZORAN: I took up a position in Bulgaria. Dragana and I were engaged and she moved to Bulgaria with me. We married six months later. To live in that country she had to learn how to ski which was a big challenge, both for her and for me!

DRAGANA: Because we moved out of Yugoslavia, Zoran became not only my husband and my lover, he was also my brother and my best friend. We had to depend on each other and we are now much closer than we would have been if we had stayed in Yugoslavia. I don't think our relationship would be as intense.

ZORAN: We were in Bulgaria for three years. We moved back to Belgrade, but then I was asked to go back to Bulgaria for another year. Dragana was pregnant with our second baby so it didn't make sense for all of us to move. It made sense for her to be surrounded by our parents and friends. I commuted each weekend to Belgrade and back. It was 400 kilometres one way. It wasn't much fun, but we knew it would only be for one year.

DRAGANA: I was pregnant and although I had all the support you could imagine back home, I didn't have Zoran. I talked to Zoran every day and he knew every single thing, but it still wasn't like having him there. In the future I would go with him wherever he went. I would never be apart from him again.

ZORAN: No one was expecting what happened in 1999. One Monday I returned to Bulgaria just as normal. But then the Americans started bombing Yugoslavia on Wednesday so I couldn't go back and my family couldn't move out. Our youngest was only two weeks old then and she didn't have a passport. The police stations had been shut down and everyone was seeking shelters. It was very frightening. I remember talking to Dragana on the phone and at the other end I could hear the emergency sirens and Dragana was saying she had to go. It was a shock. You don't want to believe it.

I had a few sleepless nights and finally, through some connections, got them out. When we were in Bulgaria Dragana and I made the decision not to go back to Belgrade in the short term and we looked at our options. I was offered a very nice ex-pat package in the Ukraine. It was a big country with great potential and it would have been a great job, but Dragana wasn't happy.

DRAGANA: It sounded beautiful. But money can't buy you health and there were also security issues. I would have had to have a driver to take me everywhere. It is the wild, wild east over there.

ZORAN: There was a position available in New Zealand. I had an interview and I was offered the job and here we are five years later. It is one of the best decisions we have ever made. I was in Belgrade a few weeks ago and I was able to think about the advantages and disadvantages of being here or being there. We are here and we love it. We will always have our accent, but our kids will have the Kiwi accent instead and we are very happy about that.

The beautiful girl in the window is now my wife. I had been looking for someone like her for 35 years. Dragana is a combination of everything a man would ever try to find. Good-looking, optimistic, honest and open, and ready to share.

DRAGANA: I thought I was an optimist until I met Zoran, but I am nothing compared with him. He is positive all the time. There are no problems for him. We went through a time where there were shortages of certain products we couldn't buy. Zoran is such a practical guy and he looked after these things. I never had to worry. I want to grow old with him. I don't imagine being with anyone else but him.

Dragana, 36; Zoran, 46

Fun times

We total 2 – That's quite okay
for such a ha ha day
walking down the Parade
to the floodgates
opened by a southerly

Alan Brunton

A relationship can be a lot of fun. It might be the simple pleasures of a lazy Sunday brunch together, a walk on the beach or making jokes while you both prepare a meal. It might be a shared hobby or sport. Or it might be projects like building a house together or travelling the world. Whatever you do, create your own unique adventures together. Open yourself to your partner as they grow and express different sides of themselves. And be excited about being open to the unexpected: when you do this, love turns from juice to sparkling champagne.

I love Jon dearly. We have been together for six years and life with him is always an adventure. I never know what he is going to dream up next. A month ago he followed me around for a day with a camera. He told me he was making a photo essay of my life. I'm pretty relaxed around cameras, but told him it was only okay if I got to follow him around the following weekend. It was such a fun experience. A little wacky I suppose but we learnt a lot about each other — and we now have this wonderful visual record.

Harriet, 32

We can't seem to help ourselves because every birthday we can't resist playing funny pranks on each other. My husband is a high school teacher so for his last birthday myself and two friends marched into his school dressed in (tasteful) suspenders, short dresses and feather boas. We strode into his class mid-lesson and performed a karaoke number to 'Hey, Big Spender' and then we sang 'Happy Birthday'. My husband was the colour of the red balloons we had brought along with us, although I know he loved the attention. It was great!

Jessica, 27

We like to hit the highway on our bikes — all my surfing and kayaking gear has been growing cobwebs since I bought Jean her own machine. Oh, and nooky . . . with motorbikes, one thing often leads t'other. Good, eh?

Bruce, 56 (he said in a small voice)

My husband makes living with him a romantic adventure. I sometimes come home and there will be rose petals scattered on the bed and champagne open by the bath tub. This is not something I would always appreciate, but he is wonderfully sensitive and always seems to know when I am in the mood for romance OTT.

Susan, 44

Getting through the hard times

Nothing is more beautiful than the love that has weathered the storms of life.

Jerome K. Jerome

We would never welcome difficult times in our lives, but hard times stretch us beyond our limits and can expand our love. By consoling our partner we can help them feel less alone if tragedy strikes. The grind of everyday life also provides challenges as well. The road of love can be filled with the potholes of money worries, household duties, health scares, difficult children or in-laws – but try not to detour. Just love each other, support each other, let the journey unfold and try not to worry unnecessarily.

I think too many people read romantic books that give them the wrong idea about love.

Jaimie, 10

For many years we had to work hard as we were married just at the end of the Great Depression. To keep the farm we had to go without quite a lot, but it drew us closer together. Life was not a bed of roses. There were good times and not-so-good times. But through it all there was the feeling of our togetherness.

Jean, 86

When my mother died, Lorraine was always there for me being supportive, but also allowing me any space I required in order to deal with my own grief and all the other demands which crop up at those times. She made the grieving process as simple as it could possibly be. She partnered me through it. I hope I can be as supportive for her when that bridge is crossed.

Terry, 57

We have relocated a few times since the birth of our first child. That in itself is stressful. Our first move to the States was particularly tough. It was different to most things we had known, but having a young child, getting pregnant and then going through post-natal depression would send most men off in a tizz. But Neil was my rock. We definitely have a stronger marriage after going through our ups and downs in the States. It is lucky in our case we had a history and we are best friends first.

Mandy, 30s

Over the last year I've had two miscarriages. This is something that has been very hard for both of us. Being an emotional person one of the ways I deal with grief is to cry. A lot of men would have found that hard but Roger has been really good. He has also had his own grief to deal with. We had only known each other 18 months when I had the second miscarriage. I guess a lot of marriages would have failed. I'm sure that our love for each other and the desire to make our marriage work have helped us cope and draw closer.

Joy, 42

I wasn't able to extricate myself from a relationship that got too romantically heavy for me at the time: every time I tried to bug out, the waterworks got turned on. I couldn't stand her misery; we got married. Now there's a good recipe for 'they lived happily ever after', eh? Not! It was inevitable that I would have to work out how to be married and how to be friends with the woman 'after the bath water cooled'.

Incredible as it may seem, we did manage to stay together, we did sort out a lot of the issues in both our pasts, and we did manage to look after our kids – until the first-born hit his teen years. When it became imperative to really start with some tough parenting, it was the last straw for my wife. All the progress we had made over the years came unglued. Things were so bad that I showed her the door of the house and invited her to put herself on the other side of it. That put her so far down in the hole that she got some badly needed professional help, I was able to straighten the kids out a bit, and after 14 months we reconstituted the family with a new set of contracts and undertakings between the family members.

My wife is now less romantic, more loving (and lovable), and is willing to assist me with 'tough love' when necessary. She withdraws into her own shell (previously her favourite defence) much less often. Her romantic image of me appears to have been replaced by one that is much closer to the real me, so I have less unreal expectations to have to try and fulfil. Our sometimes reluctant partnership has, by some mysterious process, grown into a loving marriage.

Bruce, 50s

A special story of love

Always, there are our hearts
to consider.
They are most
precious to us.

Jenny Bornholdt

Paula's first husband, Pat, suffered an aneurysm, and he gave his blessing for her to marry again. Together, Paula and her second husband, Erik, cared for Pat. This is their extraordinary story of love.

I met Pat in Dunedin when he was boarding with our neighbour. There was a gate between the two houses and the neighbour used to come over and Pat got in the habit of coming over too. Pat loved his cup of tea. He was nine years older than me and was a sophisticated person. I was 17 and was used to teenage boys so he was a breath of fresh air. We were friends for some time. He actually asked Mum if he could take me out initially because he was older.

On the first date he took me out to dinner and then we started seeing each other on a regular basis. I think our association really began in earnest when he went to Australia and I went over and stayed with him and his flatmate. Up until then I hadn't been sure that he was the right man for me. To cut a long story short we came back to New Zealand, went to Napier and our daughter, Teressa, was born there. And then we went to Dunedin. I was 20. We didn't get married until 9 years later, but there was never any question that we were a couple.

Pat was so wonderful. He had an extremely high IQ. He was a social animal and was a lot of fun. I felt a wee bit in awe of him initially, although he always encouraged me. He always said, whatever I wanted to do, to go for it. We were soul mates. We did everything together – and Teressa and her father were extremely close.

When Pat was 42 he had an aneurysm. I was 33. We were living in Oamaru and went to Dunedin Hospital to have this confirmed. For one week he was able to move and talk, although he wasn't right, but then he went into a semi-coma. He couldn't speak and he was paralysed for weeks and weeks. The doctors were amazed because whenever I walked into the room he turned his head, but that was all he could do. After eight weeks he was still in Dunedin Hospital and the doctors were concerned with me driving back and forth during winter, so he was moved to Oamaru.

I visited Pat every day and along with Teressa, friends and family, we taught him to move one finger. Then he managed to hold a spoon up to his mouth. It was a long haul. It took us 12 months to get this movement, but we got there. He slowly gained use of one arm. The first emotional response we got from Pat was when my half-sister played the piano for him. It was like he was crying, but he was happy. Before then there was no emotion at all because he couldn't show it. That was a breakthrough: the music.

I was transferred to Christchurch with my work and I transferred Pat to be near us. I met Erik at work. Erik plays the guitar so I asked him to come with me to the hospital one day and he played the guitar for Pat. We had a party for Pat. By this stage Pat could get around the hospital in a wheelchair and he knew everyone. Even as a sick man he was a social person. So Erik played guitar for Pat and Pat got to know Erik that way. We always looked for ways to occupy Pat. He was a very intelligent man, bored out of his brain, locked in a body he couldn't move apart from some use of one arm.

During this time I was invited out lots of times by married couples, all friends I had known for many years. But then I got to the stage where I was tired of always going out as a single woman. I was invited to a function and asked Erik if he would go with me. We were also part of the social club at work so that is how we got to be friends.

Over a long period of time Erik and I became close and we talked about getting married. We had to consider Pat. I talked to my daughter and she was happy, so one day I spoke to Pat and I said, 'Erik and I thought we might get married. How do you feel about that?'

Pat said, 'If you have to do that I'm glad it is Erik. He is the person I would choose for you.'

Erik and I were bringing Pat home for dinner not long after that and I got out of the car to open the doors. We hadn't spoken to Pat together, so it was a big shock when Pat turned to Erik and said, 'I understand you want to marry my wife.' Erik said, 'Ah . . . yes.' Pat said, 'Why?' And Erik said, 'Because I love her', and Pat said that was a good enough reason for him and gave Erik his blessing.

Pat knew that we would never leave him and Erik knew that Pat was part of my life. If he married me he had Pat too. The three of us understood that, and our families and our friends understood. Erik loved all of us. And Pat loved Erik.

From the family point of view Pat had a full life because he was part of a family and he also inherited Erik's family. Whenever there was a function, Pat was invited to it, no questions asked, and he always came. In the early days we didn't have access to wheelchair taxis so we always had to go and pick him up, which was heavy going, but we did it.

Pat died in 2002. Teressa and I sat with him constantly the last three weeks of his life. Erik sat with him too. He had been sick for 19 years. I miss him. I actually lost him twice – once when he got sick and then when he died.

Erik is a great guy and was brilliant with Pat. Pat was like his brother and he wanted that conveyed at the funeral. The four of us, Pat, Erik, Teressa and myself, were a family – albeit an unusual family – but still a family. Teressa always said if and when she got married she wanted Erik to push Pat down the aisle so they would both be there together.

Paula, 50s

Love that grows

In love, what do we love
But to give and to receive
That love by which we live.

Charles Brasch

There are three people in an intimate relationship: 'I', 'you' and 'us'. Take care of all three, and allow yourselves to develop and grow as individuals and as a couple. Your partner may want to do yoga once a week, or study towards a qualification, or take up tennis — and you may not want to do these things yourself. Encourage them in these pursuits; let them be themselves and have their freedom. At the same time find common things to experience together. With love and understanding the 'us' you have created together will grow stronger as time goes by.

I think Sarah's job was a good way for the two of us to start a marriage. She was working for Air New Zealand and when we first married I lived on my own 21 nights a month. I had been married before but then I'd had the freedom and the space. Sarah was independent and quite goal orientated, so for the two of us to be stuck together all the time straight away might have come as a shock. After a year Sarah said she would give up flying internationally. She got a job on the domestic service so she was home much more. I wondered what it would be like and six months later, I thought, yeah this is cool. The time had flown by and it was the first I had thought about it.

Richard, 42

We have known each other for more than 16 years and we love each other more now than when we were teenagers. Mathew has encouraged me to follow my dream of being a musician, even though this is something that often causes me to travel and be apart from him. I've encouraged him in his sport, even though I'm not a sporty person. By doing this our love for each other has grown immensely.

Melissa, 32

Trust is the most important thing in a marriage. We talk about everything we do, what we are going to do and how we are going to do it. We have individual pursuits, but we also do many things together. And as far as we are concerned it is the things we achieve together that are the most important over a long period of time. Over the years our love has grown.

Earline, 60s

When I was younger I met men and instantly fell in lust – but I never had a real friend. When I went flatting with Daniel he became a friend. We shared similar backgrounds and we had the same hopes and aspirations. He never expected me to be anything other than what I was. He is a man who doesn't like pretence. It was really hard but I was myself – and he still liked me! So our relationship was built on our friendship; love came afterwards.

Love didn't come in a blinding flash. It came quite by surprise. I came up for a holiday when he moved to

Auckland a couple of years after we first met. He saw me off at the airport and he gave me a little kiss to say goodbye. All of a sudden another possibility popped up into my head. I had to chase him. He'd come out of a marriage that had been very unhappy and he wasn't sure if he was ready for it.

We lived together for a couple of years but then we split up. He really needed to spread his wings. I had travelled overseas in my 20s but he hadn't. He was restless and I could see that. His aunty died and left him a couple of thousand dollars. I suggested he went overseas and do his thing. So he went. I knew I would never love anyone as much as Daniel – but I was prepared to let him go. And I thought, 'That is love.' If he didn't come back at least I'd had something I never thought I was capable of having. But he came back and we got married in 1982. I think love is letting people be who they are and giving them that freedom. I have such respect and such feeling for Daniel – and vice versa, I know. We have a solid commitment to each other. Like two swans who pair up for life.

Laura, 50s

The love story of a marriage

Life is too short for our love even though we stayed together every moment of all the years.

Katherine Mansfield, in a letter to her husband John Middleton Murray

A widow talks about the special love she shared with her husband over 26 years.

John did the Kiwi OE. He went to Indonesia and from there he travelled to Singapore. I was 19 and working at the doctor's clinic as a receptionist. He was a commercial diver and he had to come in and get injections for yellow fever, smallpox and all that. So we met over the counter in the doctor's office! He asked me out, but I said 'No' because I didn't know him. I thought he was a very happy person because he was always smiling, but he had to ask me out quite a few times before I said 'Yes'.

During Chinese New Year, Eurasian girls like me work while the Chinese have time off. John asked me out for dinner, but I said I didn't want to go out because Chinese New Year was so crowded. He said, 'Can I just come over and see you?' I said 'Okay', so our first date was at home with my mum.

I was 21 when we married; he was three years older. We had a small wedding, but that was all I wanted. We got married in St Teresa's Church and we only filled two of the pews! But it was really beautiful; the day was just lovely.

We moved to New Zealand the following year. It was a huge change. I couldn't wait to come to New Zealand. John had told me so many stories. I instantly loved the fresh air and the countryside – although he didn't tell me how cold it would be! It took me two years to get used to the weather. But New Zealand is beautiful and right from the start I loved it. It was a very exciting time. Everything was such an adventure.

I truly loved John. I loved that he cared for me, that he provided security and that he loved me. I was so, so sure that he loved me before all else. He was my steady rock. Throughout our time together John always did things that were lovely. If I didn't want to do any grocery shopping he would go and do that for me. When I was pregnant with our second child I was very ill so he did all the cooking. Then when I was eight months pregnant, I tripped and fell and I tore the ligaments in my pelvis. I was put into hospital right up until I gave birth six weeks later. All that time he looked after our eldest daughter by himself. He juggled caring for her, visiting me and working. I don't know how he managed.

Not having family nearby made us very self-sufficient. We just had each other. We had to get on and that was it.

Sometimes my eldest daughter will compare her relationships to what John and I had. She will say, 'But Dad used to do this for you, and Dad used to do that.' I will tell her that she is looking at us after we had had many years together. She didn't see us when we first started, when we were learning to cope with each other.

We had different religions; we had different backgrounds. One example is that when I was growing up my family pampered us when we were sick, but John had been brought up differently. If you were sick you had to go to bed and go to sleep. If you were well enough to talk then you should be at school. As you can imagine, we had fights about this when it came to our own daughters. We learnt to compromise. Sometimes we would follow his way, sometimes mine. In the end it was the meeting of the two. But at first we weren't able to make these compromises. It was either my way or the door! I used to have quite a temper; my Portuguese fiery side would come out. But when I'd calmed down John would talk me through things. He was very good at doing that.

We were totally in love with each other and we were very committed to having a good marriage. Towards the last few years of being together we had grown so close that we could finish each other's sentences. We often knew what the other was thinking just with a look. The last six years of his life were the best years for us. When we first started we were very in love but it was difficult. As we got older our love wasn't as intense but it was deeper. The relationship became more real. And as individual people we grew a lot within our marriage. Perhaps that is a key to a happy marriage.

John was 48 when he died. He died the day before our 24th wedding anniversary. That was tough. I don't know that I cope well without him. I was in a bad way the first couple of years, but now I'm getting better. I push myself to do things. I sold our house – that was a big step. And I'm now working, which is good. I know John would want me to try and be positive. It is four years now since he died, but after being married for 24 years and knowing him for 26 years, it is not long.

Karen, late 40s

Looking towards the future

The future belongs to those who believe in the beauty of their dreams.

Eleanor Roosevelt

One of the nicest things about being a couple is being able to dream and plan and think about the future together. It might be having children, building a house or travelling. It might be developing a business together. Whatever the dream, two people with the same vision are a powerful team.

Brad and I talk about our dreams and aspirations all the time. Even if life doesn't go according to our plans I love that we can share our hopes together.

Ellen, 25

We have a lot of fun talking about the future together. We are planning to travel extensively in a couple of years, but after that we would like to buy a lifestyle block, have a few chickens and some sheep and a cow or two and live the simple life.

Camellia, 37

My husband and I have always talked about working together and running our own business. It's taken years of planning but we have finally taken the leap. We have bought a motel down south. We have only been running it six months but we love living our dream.

Marlene, 41

Our hope for the future is a long and happy life together. We have always said we would like to sit on the porch on a swing when we are old. Just to hold hands and be together. We didn't think we could have kids, so the dream was never to sit there and watch our grandchildren play. But now we have children we'd like to be old enough to see them married off with kids of their own.

Sarah, 38

I feel different since I got married. I can't explain it, but it is like our relationship has gone to a whole new level. It is a feeling of commitment and there is a lovely feeling of belonging. I feel so happy I have found the right person. He is my partner and my best friend. There is nothing I don't love about Andrew. He is kind, sincere, honest, loyal and he's calm. He loves me to bits. My hope for the future is for us to not ever lose what we've got – and hopefully to have a couple of kids. I want us to grow together. If we continue to be who we are, if we continue to be honest and appreciate one another and not take each other for granted, I think we will be okay.

Sonia, early 30s

Expressions of love

Affirming words

Lovelier are her words
Than the exquisite notes
That speak the souls of flutes.
The song of birds.

A. R. D. Fairburn

Words are relationship food. They feed love and nourish the spirit, so be generous with your words. Affirming words pile up like snowflakes to create a blanket of love, so praise your lover often. Tell your partner that you love them – and be specific about what you love about them. You can do this verbally and you can also put your thoughts down on paper. There is nothing that pulls at the heartstrings more than an old-fashioned love letter.

One thing he said to me when we first met was, 'Everything I have ever wanted in a woman I can see through your eyes.' It sounds corny but it wasn't a line. He was actually being genuine. We have been together ever since and we married last year.

Sonia, early 30s

He often tells me he loves me but it's not just what he says, it's how he says it too. He often says words of reassurance to boost my lack of confidence.

Nikki, 33

Keith often tells me that he loves my creativity and my drive. I am an artist and his words give me a lot more confidence than I would have otherwise. He makes me feel very secure and loved.

Alison, 27

Susie always says a lot of encouraging things about the job that I do. It makes me feel good going to work each day knowing she appreciates my hard work. I love her for that.

John, 38

Michael often says, 'I love you.' However, he has a whole range of sub-verbal sounds, faces, little acts and pantomimes that are often more expressive than what he says: it makes me feel loved and it also makes me laugh.

Kat, 31

Whenever one of us has to go away overnight we leave behind a letter to the other on the kitchen table. Some letters are only a few lines; others have gone on for pages. We have kept all these letters, and twenty years on they are a beautiful document of our love for each other.

Marsha, 52

Physical closeness

Drowning is easy, my darling,
As when foundering lip to lip
Horizons topple and vanish
And into your breathing I slip.

Alistair Te Ariki Campbell

If sex in an intimate relationship is champagne, then affection is hot chocolate. It is the simple things like holding hands, kissing and cuddling that allow us to soak in the warm comfort of each other. Naturally, sensitivity is required. Not everyone likes to be touched in the same way but if it is mutually pleasing it helps keep our love tanks full. As well as making love, it can be the small gestures – the brief caress of your partner's back in the kitchen, the loving kiss and cuddle before going to work – that communicate love powerfully.

People kissing grosses me out at this age but it might be something I want to try when I am older. It might be okay.

Lizzie, 10

I enjoy spontaneous cuddles, hugs, smooches and pash-ups. It sure is hard not to get the message you are loved when this happens.

Terry, married for 12 years

It makes me feel loved when my husband reaches for me in the night for cuddles. We enjoy quality time in bed. Holding hands in bed is an added closeness. And he is still grabbing certain parts of me – at our age!

Diana, married for more than 41 years

We often hold hands in the evening when we are watching TV, or give each other unexpected cuddles – like when we are both staring at the toaster waiting for it to pop up!

Joy, 50s

The first time we made love it was astonishing. It was indescribably wonderful, which was a big surprise to me as I'd never really liked sex that much before. To be honest, I wondered why people made such a big deal about it. We had been friends for a number of years and our relationship slowly turned into love. We trust each other so I think we brought a great deal of emotional and spiritual intimacy to our relationship before we became physically close. We have now been married for 11 years and our love-making is a true blessing to me. It makes me feel incredibly loved and satisfied – not only physically, but in a soul way too.

Rebecca, 39

She is my lover and my best friend. When we make love time stands still. It is like there is no beginning and no end. I am totally lost in just whatever she and I want, with no inhibitions; we are just in the moment and at one with the universe. We are completely and utterly absorbed in one's object of love, to the point of merging into one life force.

Max, 48

In my first marriage my husband was physically abusive and it has taken me a long while to learn to trust another man, especially with my body. I am fortunate to have met a wonderful man who I love very much. He is sensitive, gentle and very kind. We have been married now for three years. I love that he cuddles me often and that he is very receptive to how I am feeling. At first sex was still a 'closed off' experience for me but as time has gone on and I trust my husband more I find I am beginning to enjoy it. And I love being held afterwards.

Alana, 34

I still am amazed at how special making love is – every time! Each time, it is the most amazing experience, exhilarating and almost spiritual, as it is so intimate. Even if it is not as often as when I was first married, it has less of the urgency of young love and more of the deeper, richer expressions that relationships grow into. There is something very special in physical closeness, a hug, a kiss, a caress, a cuddle and making love itself, and in knowing someone that intimately. I love the lingering glow of warmth, lying together.

Jen, married 25 years

Gift-giving

Such flowers are never seen except by lovers, and then — rarely — rarely.
I have put them all in the big jar and they are on the table before the mirror.
You will never know what joy they have given me.

Katherine Mansfield, in a letter to her husband John Middleton Murray

Most wedding ceremonies involve the giving and receiving of rings as a symbol of love. And in day-to-day life, gifts are a wonderful, visual way to show your lover that you care. So don't be reluctant to buy your partner a gift — but do bear in mind the most precious gifts are about love and thoughtfulness and have nothing to do with their price tag.

My favourite gift was when he brought some wild clematis from the back of the farm and put it in a jar on top of the bookcase.

Jean, 86

Our dog was recently killed in a pack attack; she had been the last of my working dogs before we moved to town. Grief was pretty maximal. My wife commissioned a friend of hers to do a portrait of said hound, and had it mounted and framed for my birthday. I was right chuffed.

Bruce, 56

There is one thing I gave Sarah that I am really proud of. When I moved to Auckland a friend and I set up a small building company so I was self-employed for the first time. From my first cheque I bought Sarah a watch that I wouldn't have been able to save up to buy. It was cool because it was the first cheque for doing something for me rather than working for someone else. It was early on in our relationship. And I know the watch is special to Sarah. It hasn't come off her wrist in years.

Richard, 42

I used to buy Eleanor lots of little gifts, but when we got married I stopped doing that because I thought we couldn't afford it. But then one day I remembered how much she had enjoyed me buying her little gifts, so I started coming home with small things for her again. A rose one night, another night some chocolates. I know they are all traditional things – I'm not a creative chap – but Eleanor tells me she feels very loved when I give her small things. And if your wife feels loved that is a very good thing!

Doug, 64

My husband recently gave me a CD he had put together containing a compilation of music he thought I would enjoy for the car. It was a great selection of music and I appreciated the effort.

Catherine, 35

Kind deeds

I can't get past the way I feel for you
It's the little things that make this worth the effort
It's the small, little, insignificant things you do.

Brooke Fraser

True love lives in the real world and it knows that everyday tasks still need to be done. But by doing chores with an attitude of love you can turn everyday things such as cooking, housework and picking up the kids into an expression of love. Burdens are shared and it is often the little thoughtful things that you do that make your partner feel loved the most.

I only have to mention something requires fixing and it is done. And he always is happy and contented, singing or whistling while he is at home and as he helps me.

Diana, 50s

I am lucky. He does washing, cleaning and dishes and generally helps around the house. I know a lot of men don't do that. I appreciate him for doing that and I am grateful that he does.

Joy, 42

If it is Friday night and she offers to shout pizza instead of me having to cook, that'll do.

Bruce, 56

My wife is wonderful. She cooks a couple of nights a week even though I know she doesn't enjoy it much. I'm a chef so tend to do all the other cooking at home. It's really great that she knows I need to have a break from it sometimes and willingly takes over. This is one of the many things that she does that shows she loves me. It doesn't matter what she cooks, or what the food is like. It is just the fact that she cares to take over on occasion.

Ed, 33

My husband is a teacher. When it is school holiday time he tries to do all the cooking and housework so that I have a break from it. I am working part time now; I try to do as much as I can on my two days off so that he can get his school work done and we have time together at the weekends.

Joy, 50s

My partner is really loving and kind. I've gone back to school and am doing some study. Every night Tom sits down at the end of the evening and 'tests' me on what I have learnt that day. It really helps me – and it also makes me feel good that he takes such an interest in what I'm doing.

Fiona, 43

Quality time

Come out of the circle of time
And into the circle of love.

Rumi

Spending quality time together is crucially important in an intimate relationship. Without time together people can become strangers; love can wither and die. So take time out from the everyday bustle of life to spend some undivided time together, whether it is at home or out. You might enjoy going out to dinner and talking for hours. You might prefer walking on the beach at sunset. You might want to put on some music and stay at home and chat. Do something both you and your lover will enjoy; build a sense of togetherness and give each other space to talk openly and honestly.

I like to do things with my husband. I think it is so important to be friends as well as lovers. We like to have a few beers, listen to some music, see our friends, travel, shop and do things around the house.

Nikki, 33

We both enjoy bush-walking and getting away from phones. We enjoy kite-flying at the beach and in the local reserves. And we enjoy reading books. Although we both read different types of books, we read together in the same room.

Joy, 42

One of our most enjoyable achievements was our three-month OE in '91. We got to spend all that time together as we went around Europe and the UK. It brought us closer together as a couple. We were both looking at our roots and we got so much joy out of each other's exciting discoveries.

Earline, 60s

We enjoy going into Wellington City and looking at art galleries. We are both interested in interior design and so we both enjoy looking at furniture stores and fabrics. We like to go walking – both to keep fit and enjoy the scenery. Walking along Petone Beach is one of our favourite things to do, then going and having a coffee or a meal somewhere. We enjoy picnics in the summer.

Joy, 50s

Each week-night when Spencer comes home from work we pour a glass of wine and we sit and chat about our day. We usually spend half an hour like this before we consider doing anything else, like housework or cooking or spending time with the kids. Our children are now used to this routine and know that they will have time with us after Mummy and Daddy have had time together. We put our relationship first – and I think that is a good thing to do.

Jasmine, 31

Storgé

FAMILY LOVE

It is the absurdity of family life, the raggedness of it, that is at once its redemption and its true nobility.

James McBride

Storgé is the Greek word for family love that includes affection and maternal instinct. Families – whanau in New Zealand – do not come pre-packaged in a standard shape or size. Every one of us has a unique family life with its own challenges. There is no such thing as a perfect family – whatever outward appearances – but there is such a thing as a loving family. Life is no longer as simple as it was. Society and technology are more sophisticated and less family-orientated. But families are the backbone of our society and it is important that they not just exist, but thrive. Historian Edward Gibbon identified the main reasons for the decline and fall of the Roman Empire and number one on his list was the breakdown of family structure. Families matter: they are our teachers and sculptors. Good or bad, their influence shapes us for a lifetime.

Creating a loving, safe and supportive environment is the most important function of a family. Everyone needs somewhere they can be vulnerable and open without fear of recrimination. And it is important to have family time and bonding experiences. Each family creates a unique culture, with their own beliefs, attitudes and traditions. But, however diverse these mini-communities, happy families have common attributes. Family members are kind. They don't put each other down. They apologise rather than refusing to say they are sorry. If they make promises they keep them. And they forgive each other rather than holding grudges and nurturing grievances.

Passing down the lessons you have learned is a natural part of being a parent or grandparent. In this way the circle of life and love continues and wisdom is passed down the generations. And even if you arrive at the portal of parenthood badly deprived of good parenting yourself, your children's love to you is a gift. With a willing heart you can break bad cycles and create a new environment of love. Parents, love your children – especially when they are young. They have no-one else but you to love them when they are small and vulnerable. Their life is in your hands.

Through hard times and good times families are tied together by ropes stronger than the strands of DNA. Families are bound together by the ropes of love, the fastenings of compassion and the ties of a common, caring humanity. Loving whanau is the most precious endowment of humanity. And loving families are our hope for the future.

Mums

I want everyone to know that my mum is the best. She is my best friend. I have lots of buddies, but my mum beats them all. She has stuck by me all my life and she is 100% reliable in her loyalty. Thank you Mum, I love you.

Message on New Zealand Mother's Day website

A mother's love for her child is a powerful force, an emotional bond stronger than iron and steel. Nurturing, moulding, shaping: a mother's care for her children often begins before they are born and continues for a lifetime. Through teething troubles, scraped knees and homework woes, from teenage angst to a relationship reborn into adulthood, the unconditional love of a mother is one of the most precious gifts to the human race.

I am pregnant with my second child and I am a bit worried as you get so used to the first child and the way they behave. The second child could be completely different and I will have to learn everything again. I can't imagine loving a child as much as I love Jack, but I am sure when the baby arrives I will love him or her as much.
Kerry, 30s

I would like to tell of the love my daughter, Kendall and I share. Kendall has Down's Syndrome and her capacity to love and to be loved is no different from any other child.

> I love her compassion and ability to empathise with others.
> I love her quirky sense of humour.
> I love her total acceptance and non-judgmental attitude.
> I love her ability to live the moment.
> I love early morning cuddles in bed with Kendall.
> I respect her perseverance.
> I love her total lack of competitiveness.
> I love watching her play and interact with her older siblings.
> I love watching her dance.
> I love the pure magic that makes Kendall the unique and beautiful person she is.

Diane, mother of 12-year-old Kendall

I love the look on my children's faces every day when I collect them from daycare and school. They are always happy to see me, no matter how bad their day has been.
Mandy, mother of a 4-year-old and a 9-year-old

Mother love is something I never expected to have. I always thought I'd be off travelling the world as a free spirit or climbing the corporate ladder, but when I found out, at the age of 21, that I was expecting Elisabeth, the die was cast. Watching that tiny baby emerge and having her placed in my arms was quite overwhelming.

There wasn't an instant bond – more a curiosity at this wee being that had been turning my insides out over the preceding months. We looked at each other and I said, 'Welcome to the world.' From that moment I knew I had to change because my needs were no longer paramount: here was this tiny baby so completely dependent on Tim and me to survive. Over the weeks, months and years to follow an overwhelming love for all three of my daughters has emerged.

Sonia, 30s

There is something magical about raising children. You have to go through the experience to understand. All you can do is keep loving them. It is just like a washing machine, where it goes round and round. You simply have to be there throughout the cycle for when they come out at the end.

Hirawa, mother of five children; the youngest is 31

My children give my life more worth. I have a sense of accomplishment and wellbeing by marrying the man that I did, but when I had my children it was a personification of the love we have in our marriage.

Lucy, 50s

My four children are all grown-up and now have children of their own. They are all capable, caring people and I am very proud of them. But I still worry about them and pray every day for their wellbeing. I have been a mother too long to stop.

Audrey, 69

A mother's love

Making the decision to have a child — it's momentous. It is to decide forever to have your heart go walking outside of your body.

Elizabeth Stone

A mother talks about the special love she has for her children.

I always wanted to have children. I don't think I thought about the reason; I just always did. It was something that was natural. The first time you hold your child in your arms is really difficult to describe because it is like nothing you have ever felt before. It is probably the first time you feel absolute true love. It always makes me feel emotional just thinking of it. This doesn't happen with everyone but for me the love was instantaneous. When I had our second child, Jessica, I was concerned that I wouldn't love her as much as I did our eldest, Jane. But when I had Jessica I realised I didn't have a limit on love.

The love you feel is a warm enveloping feeling. You have this tiny little person who is absolutely dependant on you so it is quite scary as well. I think I was lucky having my children when I was young. It was like having dolls to play with. I didn't have any fears about whether I should have them, or how motherhood would fit into my career or anything like that. It was simple. We wanted to have kids so we did.

Being a mother has definitely changed me. I think it has made me more emotional. I've spoken to a few mothers about this and they find the same thing. I feel I have more caring for things like animals and children in general. I think it has made me more tolerant.

I love different things about my daughters. I love Jane's sense of fun. It is nice she doesn't feel like she needs to grow up and change. That is really important because if she started losing her sense of fun she would lose her personality and it would go against the grain. I love and admire Jessica's constant determination to give 110% of herself to anything and anyone she touches. If something is important to her, nothing will stop her from achieving her goals. When you have a friend in either of our girls you have a friend for life. They are not fickle. They are loyal and very loving.

Your relationship with your children does change as they go through different ages. The first few years are spent basically looking after them because they can't look after themselves. But then you have to break that tie and allow them to do things. You teach them to stand on their own two feet. When they go to school you are still nurturing them but that is when the first piece of string gets broken.

They grow up all of a sudden and they change from babies to little people. Then you survive them being teenagers. Our kids weren't bad. I think we were very lucky. But girls are moody and there were lots of slammed doors and screams and yells. They would say 'I hate you' and all that kind of stuff. I don't think you get that as much with boys. They were normally 'hating' you because you had told them they couldn't do something. So there are reasons behind their anger and I don't think it actually hurts you when they say these things. It is interesting because during the different stages of their growing up Jessica was very loving when Jane wasn't and Jane was very loving when Jessica wasn't.

I have many special memories of my daughters over the years. I used to like to watch the girls express themselves. Both of them used to make us laugh. Jessica used to love dressing up. They had a dress-up box and Jessica used to come out in the funniest things. She was always a quiet little thing where Jane was the noisy one and always making up cute words. Jane was very sweet and protective of her little sister. There were a lot of good times.

My kids have definitely been a comfort in sad times. When I was in hospital a few years ago Jessica would come and just sit beside the bed and be there, which was really nice. Jane did as well, but Jessica spent more time with me because she had more time to spend. When my husband's mother died and when my mother died, the girls were really supportive. They just knew what to do. It is things like that that show me that they love me more than anything else.

I think you have to be so careful about being a friend to your kids because they actually want a mother, not a friend. I can talk to the girls like a friend can but they expect more from me because I am their mother. They expect to hear advice. They might not take it, but they expect to hear it. However, you can't plan your kids' lives. You can encourage and be there to help and support them, but it is their life and they have to make their own decisions and they have to cross their own bridges.

Some people might have expectations of what their kids will be like but I didn't. It was a big adventure. I didn't know what they were going to look like and I didn't know what they were going to be like. And as your kids are growing up you just go through the process without doing too much planning or thinking about what they might be doing in the future. You hope that they are going to be bright enough to get good jobs. But the main thing is for them to be happy and to find something they like doing.

Jessica is now 25 and Jane is 30. They are both living overseas at the moment. We speak a lot on the phone. They are always telling me that they love me. I don't know when they will come back to New Zealand, but I am looking forward to them returning. Both my girls are kind, caring people and I love them very much.
Pip, 51

Dads

Lay your head upon my shoulder
Go to sleep my little one
The days are warm the nights grow colder
Cuddle up my little one
To watch you grow, so straight and strong
The joy you bring . . .
Close your eyes, we'll be there in the morning light.

David Feehan

Never is a man more powerful than when he stoops tenderly to lift a young child. Providing, protecting and teaching, a father's love is deep and sure and strong. Many fathers also remember what it is like to be young and they enjoy playing ball games, and building Lego or train sets with their children. But, fathers make the greatest contribution when they believe in their children and encourage them.

My first child was a premmie and so it was a week or so after he was born before I was able to hold him. Having just been blessed by a full-term daughter it's really wonderful to be able to hold her within the first 20 minutes. My hope for my children is to be the people God created them to be. I would like them to be happy in what they do, and love and respect others.

Andrew, 40s

Our daughters' future is top of the priority list. I think everyone in life has at least one opportunity and you have to be skilled, educated and smart enough to grab it. If you lose an opportunity it might not happen again. I want to make sure that my children are smart enough to recognise that opportunity and they are skilled enough to grab it.

Mitchell, 42

I can never find an acceptable answer to what I love most about my family. The question seems wrong, like, 'Why do you like pain?' My boys are now (supposedly) grown men. Loving them is still tough love. I had to learn to suggest ideas and let them make their own decisions so that they could learn to understand the consequences, and it's been painful. They have far less regard for consequences than me, and will happily lock horns with all sorts of people and situations that I'd way prefer to stay out of. Perhaps I am looking across a generation gap. But if it was them or me, I'd take the fall so they could live, I know with absolute certainty. Whenever our boys are in town, they tend to head for Umupuia Beach, where their sister's ashes are scattered. We are staunch, even after death.

Bruce, married with two grown sons. His beloved daughter, Heather, died when she was nine years old.

I felt I was drifting away from my teenage son because I was away so much on business. I decided I needed to do something about this. I suggested regular outings, just the two of us, that we would work into my schedule. He immediately said yes. He dictates what we do – it is anything from ten-pin bowling to watching sports to rock climbing – and I am amazed at how well we have got to know each other by doing this. We don't go out every week, but it averages about once a week over a year. I make sure work knows about the nights out with my son. Once they are in my diary they are non-negotiable. My boss respects this and it has never been an issue.

Martin, late 40s

In my case it was a big decision to be a father as first I had to know that my illness (MS) would not be passed on to my children. I worried about them missing out on things because of my physical limitations. Kicking a ball around, tramping, riding bicycles were not an option. Fortunately, friends have stepped in over the years and given them those opportunities.

The main thing I love about my sons is how we all get along. They have never been embarrassed to be seen with the 'olds' and are still happy to go away on holiday with us. They always keep an eye on me to make sure that I am all right and often appear beside me when I am trying to cross a road so that I have an arm to grab onto. Both boys were really thrilled when they were able to take me out for a one-on-one in Wellington as they were finally big enough to push me in my wheelchair and had sufficient mass to tilt it back to get over kerbs. My health has never been an issue to them and that is something I find quite special.

I do not think I will stop officially being a father until I have got both boys into their first job and they are receiving a steady income. Then I think I will be able to step back and watch them make their own future. I would like it to be a future based on the values that we have instilled in them. I really hope that they will be able to discern the good from the bad and that they will always look for the good in people.

Patrick, 40s

A father's love

I am bright with the wonder of you
And the faint perfume of your hair.

Denis Glover

A father talks about the love he has for his two daughters, two-year-old Lola and seven-year-old Claudia, and the impact fatherhood has had on his life.

There are many different aspects to fatherhood. There is the intensity you feel when you have children. When you are growing up, love can be confusing. Do I really love someone or don't I? When you have children there is no question about the depth of emotion and the intensity you feel for them. There is no denying this is love.

When a child looks into your eyes you experience a purity that you never knew existed. When they are young, there are no hidden agendas. They live in a world where there is a joy of new discoveries. When they discover something for the first time, they experience it with glee — and it is infectious. I rediscover something at the same time.

Children also have the ability to express a whole range of emotions in the space of 10 minutes. They can be really happy and then five minutes later they are shattered and then in another five minutes they are fine. As an adult, it is hard to figure out. You are conditioned to react to certain circumstances. You might feel a certain way but you don't express it. But they don't know they are not supposed to cry at a shopping centre or laugh out loud in front of people.

Children love you, no questions asked. When they wrap their arms around you, you feel honoured and blessed. I am forever kissing the tops of my children's heads. I just can't stop myself from doing that as an expression of my love. I would gladly put my life before theirs. I begin to cork selfish emotion. I don't have a choice, because you can't be selfish when you are a father.

You spend a lot of years gathering experiences and getting material possessions, but when children come along you question if these things are what life is all about. Things I used to feel quite possessive of I have given up. I really enjoyed playing golf, but it takes all day and there is no way you can include a young child in golfing. And as a family man, I now pull back from some situations I used to find exciting. When I used to surf, sometimes it was dangerous. Now if I'm in a situation like that I get myself out of it quickly. I have a wife and two children who are relying on me, so I bear that in mind.

As a father I can't be flippant with the decisions that I make. My children are looking to me. You own their lives in a way. The things that you do can impact on their lives severely if you make the wrong decision. That is a scary awakening. In the early stages of childhood they are totally reliant on you for their lives. It is a hell of thing for someone who has always been quite carefree.

As a family we have formed a mini-community and at its nucleus are the things we do as a family. We have the parks we go to, the school we are involved in, the workplace that my family comes and visits me at. This 'tribe' that we have created has little resemblance to life BC – Before Children.

When we were expecting our first daughter, Claudia, we were oblivious in a way. We were buying prams and clothes and stuff and it was an adventure – like buying a house or getting another job. But when you witness your child being born, it is an overpowering emotion. I can't describe it. I didn't burst into tears but there was this feeling that this baby we had created was no longer a novelty. We had a child now.

When our second daughter, Lola, was born it was exciting because there was such an age gap. Claudia didn't witness Lola being born, but she was at the hospital and she came in twenty minutes later. To have our eldest child be part of the magic was really special.

Having children has made me closer to my wife. But it is a test because from a male point of view you are no longer the priority for a time. That's difficult, given the male ego. You can't blame your wife because that is just the way it is. It is a transition – but it lasts a good three years. We talked through these issues and we have a strong family network around us so that really helped. Having other people to talk to and to help us has taken some of the pressure off.

I love my daughters. I love it when Claudia comes up with something that is funny and quirky. I see aspects of myself in that. We have little jokes and tell stories together and it is really special. Another thing I love is seeing her intense happiness about something she has achieved. It might be a certificate at school, or she's managed to go across the monkey bars without falling off, or she's mastered riding a bike. To experience her joy is great.

With Lola, if I sneeze or cough, she will come up and comfort me. She'll rub my back and say, 'Are you okay, Daddy?' If Claudia falls over, Lola will start patting her. It's very genuine. To do this naturally at her age is astonishing. This is something I really love about her.

My hope is that my children will experience the fullness of life. I hope they will be motivated enough to go out there and find their own experiences, as opposed to waiting for someone else to do it for them. And I hope they will hang on to the values that we have instilled in them; that love is an important part of life; that family is important.

Nigel, 40s

Children

The family — that dear octopus from whose tentacles we never quite escape, nor in our innermost hearts, ever quite wish to.

Dodie Smith

Children are a family's future. Good parents invest time and care in their children, helping them prepare for the puzzle of life. They pass down their knowledge; they provide their children with support and they nurture their dreams. And one of the most wonderful aspects about loving children is the love they give back. Children do appreciate all that you have done for them. Some will go on and have their own families one day and so the cycle of family loving will continue.

Love from your family is so important. Too many children are born into unloving, detrimental situations these days. I've been so lucky. I believe my parents are the best parents in the world! I'm so happy, positive and confident because of the way my parents have raised me and my brother. Thanks!
Sarah, 22

I was helping my parents move the other day and was astounded at the things they still had from my childhood: paintings I had done, my old school reports, cards I had sent them and old favourite toys. I love that they have always been so interested in everything that I do.
Catlin, 22

Parents guide you and help you get through stages. They work for the money when you are not old enough to go out yourself to earn it. They give you lots of positive love. I've got a separated family. My mum has a really great sense of humour and she has passed it down to me, so we always have a good laugh. I really love that my dad is so musical and that I can talk to him about stuff.
Lizzie, 10

My parents always have good advice because they have been through stuff themselves.
Jaimie, 10

Families are important because you get knowledge from your family that is passed down to you that helps you in life, and then you pass it down to your own family.
How-Shin, 9

I will have my own family one day. I want to make sure the human race survives.
Miller, 10

Brothers and sisters

You are always in the heart — oh tucked so close there is no chance of escape — of your sister.

Katherine Mansfield, writing to her younger sister

Siblings can be a great gift to us. Shared childhoods can be a bonding experience that later translates into unconditional love in our adult lives. From the fun and the squabbles of growing up can blossom a relationship that is honest, comfortable and accepting. And when parents die, a new and much closer relationship is often forged as siblings reshape their lives without them.

You need to spend time with your brothers and sisters. This is important. My brother went away for three months. I really missed him.

Esther, 10

I didn't used to like my sister that much, but now she's moved out I can talk to her about everything – and she will always take my side. Even if I tell her about something I have done wrong, she will take my side.

Kate, 15

When my brother recently left to go to London I don't think either of us had realised how much we were going to miss each other. When we had to say goodbye we both broke down and couldn't stop crying. That's not much for me because I'm openly emotional but it was big for my brother who hardly ever cries.

Sarah, 22

My sister and I are twins. I can't imagine how people cope in life without having a twin. She is not only my sister; she is also my best friend. We are individual, different people, but we have so much in common – much more than just our physical looks. All our lives events have happened to us at the same time too. We both met our partners within the same week. We both got pregnant and had our babies only a few days apart. There has always been this synergy between us and around us. It is really special.

Tasha, 26

There are three sisters in our family. I always got on well with my younger sister, but my older sister, June, was always the popular, attractive one and I always felt the ugly duckling in comparison. It's not like that now. As you get older you get more comfortable and you accept yourself. I realise that I've got things she hasn't got and she's got things I haven't got. And there was an overnight change when Mum died. June suddenly became the matriarch in the family. Since our mother died we have all become closer as sisters.

Nicole, 49

An adoption love story

Spread love everywhere you go: first of all in your own house.

Mother Teresa

A father talks about the love he has for his adopted daughter, Sangeeta, who he first brought to New Zealand from India when she was 11 months old.

When our daughter Darshini was two years old, my wife Seetha, and I decided to investigate adopting a child. I'd had adoption at the back of my mind for some time. I felt that my life would not be complete unless I did something worthwhile, like adopting. I had an initial meeting with the Adoption Unit of Child, Youth and Family early in 1994 and in May we had decided to go ahead. An overseas adoption is dependent on a New Zealand Home Study and this took us five months to complete. Afterwards I wrote to various orphanages that were licensed to do foreign adoptions. After numerous letters and phone calls we planned our trip to India in December 1994.

We went to India only to learn the orphanages we had contacted had run out of children. An orphanage in Pune told us to come back in nine months' time and choose a baby. Seetha returned alone in August 1995. She was shown two babies and chose the younger one who had been put into the orphanage's care at birth.

Seetha came back from India with some photos. The plan was for me to go in November and bring Sangeeta back.

Up until now the process had been driven by my desire to do something worthwhile. It was quite cerebral and there wasn't much heart stuff involved. I love my own child Darshini dearly but I am not the sort of person who easily warms to other people's babies. It felt strange seeing a photo of 'my new daughter'. The photo showed Seetha holding a run-down-looking baby. The doubts started to creep in. Could I love this child?

The next two months felt surreal. There was plenty of nervous waiting and wondering. When the big day finally arrived my mind was a whirl of worried thoughts. Would I like Sangeeta? Would she like me? Would I encounter some sort of bureaucratic nightmare?

The orphanage office was an ancient, run-down building. We had to drive under a flyover bridge to enter the orphanage grounds and there were people living in rag huts under the bridge. I entered the office and Varsha, Sangeeta's social worker, introduced me around. After completing a few formalities we left by auto-rickshaw for the babies' home.

When we arrived at the building I went upstairs. Entering a room I saw a dozen metal cots. I identified Sangeeta immediately even though she had her back to me. I recognised the tight curls on her head from Seetha's photos. I could see that she had been bathed and was wearing her best dress. The instant I saw her my eyes flooded with tears and I knew that, yes, I could love her. (For most of the next week my eyes were more wet than dry!) Varsha bent over to pick her up and Sangeeta giggled and squirmed delightedly. Varsha held her towards me, Sangeeta smiled at me but leant back towards Varsha. We all sat on the floor and after half an hour Sangeeta was no longer wary. I spent a couple of hours with her, and towards the end she was happy for me to hold her and feed her a bottle.

The next morning I went to the orphanage for three hours. Sangeeta was happy to see me and not shy at all. Watching Sangeeta I could see what sort of character she was. There were two things that stood out and have remained a part of who she is. The first thing I noticed was that she often picked up small toys and turned them over and over with a concentrated look. Sangeeta is very good with her hands and takes great enjoyment out of doing or making things. Secondly, when one of the other babies cried, Sangeeta would shuffle over and try to touch them. All her life Sangeeta has been an empathetic and sociable person.

Wednesday morning was the day I 'took delivery'. I arrived at 10 a.m. and Sangeeta had been bathed and was wearing clothes I had brought from New Zealand. In the ward she naturally came to me. But as soon as we walked out of her ward she no longer seemed as happy or confident. She was frowning and clung to me. There was a small ceremony involving her caregivers then we went to the orphanage office to say goodbye. After an hour Sangeeta started to cry and clung to me for dear life – and our bond to each other was complete. By this time, even if I had wanted to, I wouldn't have been able to give her back. In the rickshaw ride back to my accommodation, Sangeeta fell asleep holding onto me. Three days later we travelled to Wellington.

The first three months with Sangeeta were quite trying. She had a distended stomach and constant diarrhoea. But it was clear from the beginning that she had a special bond with me. Every day after work she would squeal and giggle and hang onto my legs for an hour or more. Even now, nine years later, if I am sitting or lying down somewhere she will drape herself over me, or seat herself in between whoever I am sitting next to, even if it is Seetha or Darshini. Seetha and I have a private joke, that after one week of looking after Sangeeta it was obvious that she had adopted us, not that we had adopted her. She was the one in control.

I feel very privileged to have adopted Sangeeta. The process was not particularly trying. There were costs and some set backs but compared to what we have gained these are minutely insignificant. I think the hardest thing in the adoption process was the waiting. Adopting is different to the normal process of children just appearing after nine months. With adoption you have to keep moving things along. When Darshini was born I was deeply moved, but it was also a blur of emotion and tiredness. The adoption was a slow, logical and controlled process affecting different parts of my mind. I am ever thankful that the joys and disappointments of the two-year journey remain etched in a clear part of my memory.

Peter, 40s

Extended family

The family is one of nature's masterpieces.

George Santayana

Uncles. Aunties. Cousins. Nephews. Nieces. They can all help shape our lives. For those fortunate to have an extended family that are close and part of their everyday lives, the benefits can be huge: there is all that extra love and laughter to go around! But even those people without relatives close by can create their own extended family with treasured friends. So create excuses to meet regularly and enjoy the warmth, fun and support that your extended family, in whatever form, can bring to your life.

I'm an only child and with only children you can end up being a bit spoilt sometimes. So my dad and mum decided that I had to spend heaps of time with my cousins who live nearby so I learnt how to share. It's been really good because I like hanging out with them.

Lizzie, 10

I get on extremely well with the seven aunties on my mum's side of the family because they all have a fantastic sense of humour. Every time I am with any of them they are genuinely interested in my life and what I'm doing. They have a youthful spirit about them and are always up for fun. They make me feel so loved and appreciated. It is usual to see them sitting around the marae strumming their guitars and singing quietly to themselves. They will often be joined by other family members and the ease of joining in and singing together is extremely bonding. At meals we sit for hours just exchanging jokes and life experiences. There is love and acceptance when we come together.

Terehia, early 40s

My extended family is very important to me. We don't have a lot of biological family living around us, just Uncle Ray, so we have created our own circle of extended family from our friends. They have become our family. Our children call them Uncle and Aunt and we have contact regularly. We have chosen these people to be part of our lives, and part of our children's lives as a result. They are all good people. They have characteristics and traits that I admire. We hold them up to our children and say this is what they are like and this is what we respect about them: their ethics, their principles, and their morals.

Lucy, early 50s

Our whanau looks after our old people and the mentally ill. I have a cousin who has schizophrenia and is close to 60 now. For years now he has been going around the family. When it is time to move on, he just jumps in the car and goes and stays with someone else. Not only does my cousin stay with brothers and sisters, he also stays with nieces and nephews and his cousins. That is what whanau is all about. Looking after your own.

Kiri, 51

Grandparents

If nothing is going well, call your grandmother.

Italian proverb

The relationship between grandparents and their grandchildren can be a very special one. Without the same responsibilities as parents, but with the maturity and knowledge of children the second time around, grandparents have the freedom simply to enjoy their grandchildren. Often grandparents and grandchildren enjoy a quiet acceptance of each other, along with much love and laughter. This is a relationship that can be joyous fun!

I love my grandpa. He is creative and intelligent. And the thing I love about my grandmother is that she is energetic and bubbly.

Susie, 11

My grandparents have shelves covered with books and games so there is always something to do. They live close by and often pick me up after school. They are fun to be with. My other grandparents live next door so we can go over any time. They always have blocks for us to play with.

Jaimie, 10

I have never naturally been a kiddie person. If friends or family have had babies I've never had a desire to hold them and goo and gaa. But, when I had my own children I was just like every other mother and I thought I had the most beautiful babies on the face of the earth. When you have a grandchild it's very different. I keep marvelling at how I can love someone else's child so much. Everything he does is a wonder to me. I love just sitting and watching him as he discovers the world. Watching his character develop is so funny to see, little traits come out that his mother has. He isn't a cuddly baby so when he does like to cuddle and snuggle it's very difficult to hold back and not over-do it and put him off for life.

I am a lot more relaxed with this relationship. I'm more mature and far more settled within myself. Life is so much easier. Having a grandchild is a bonus.

Tracey, 43

I'm still getting used to the idea of being a grandmother, but it feels like I'm falling in love again. My granddaughter is wonderful!

Margaret, 56

One of the greatest joys of getting older is my grandchildren. It's a surprising, astonishing love.

Frank, 73

Pets

I like animals because they're honest. And I like animals because through their love comes trust, absolute and given.

Bob Kerridge

Pets are valuable members of a family. Loving us unconditionally, they lavish us with affection and bless us with their company. They bring joy to children and can become close companions to the older person. They delight us with their quirky antics and they comfort us in times of trouble just by their presence. Having a cat curled up on your lap and taking your dog for a walk on the beach on a summer's day are two of the simple pleasures in life.

My mum told me we had to get home quickly before my gift melted. I thought I was going to get a big ice cream. I went into my bedroom and I had to shut my eyes. I wondered why she made me close my eyes if it was ice cream. And then there was this squirming, wiggling furry thing: it was a little puppy! It was the best surprise ever. I've had him now for a couple of years and he is the best dog in the whole world.

Andrew, 10

The thing I love best about my cat Jazz is that she is fun. She loves chasing balls and running around the room. She also likes to sit on my lap. She has a really loud purr when I pat her.

Susie, 12

What I love most about my cat Ebony is the closeness we share and the comfort she gives me in times of trouble. Ebony is really the child I will never have. Most of my affection is poured into her (even though it is a little bit too much for her sometimes!).

Helen, mid 40s

Dogs give you unconditional love. You can come home in a bad mood and be grumpy or unkind and they will still love you. They will always forgive you.

Mike, 50s

My dog is a Jack Russell. He's named Nipper, or Nip for short, not because he bites, but because he is a little nipper. I wasn't expecting to get a puppy. It was quite a surprise. My son gave him to me not long after my wife passed away. Nip was only about three or four months old at the time. He was going around the house making little pools, like they do at that age. At first I wasn't sure about having a dog, but now he is such a member of the family. Nip is a very affectionate little dog and he is extremely smart. He is a really good little companion.

I enjoy his affection. He has a habit of lying down with his head on my foot. He follows me around everywhere; he is like a little shadow now. He will also jump up on the table and lean over and lick the side of my face.

It is the equivalent of a kiss in dog language, when they lick you like that. And he gives my ear just a little tiny gentle nip. A love nip.

He had an accident a while ago. Nip crossed the road and got run over. He's a bit more cautious now – and I keep him a lot closer. When he came home from the vet's, he had his little back leg tied up in a sling and the other leg on the front was in plaster. I thought I'd have to lift him over to his bowl and around the house. Not him! Nip just hopped around the house on two legs!

He has this habit of sitting up on his bottom with his paws up like a meerkat. I keep telling him that his grandfather must have been a meerkat. He will come in and stand like that when I am reading the newspaper. He will look me straight in the eye as if to say, 'Time for a walk'. I talk to him quite a bit. People listening in would think the old fella's gone around the twist.

We have a strong bond. He is a very faithful little dog. He's now four and we've got to know each other really well. We are living together all of the time, so naturally we have a bond. I certainly wouldn't like to do without him now. He's a great mate.

Bob, 83

Fun family times

Remember, as far as anyone knows we are a nice normal family.

Fridge magnet

Creating a fun family culture is one of the most important things any family can do – whether it is your immediate or extended family. Being able to laugh helps put life into perspective and even mundane tasks can be an adventure if humour is involved. Fun family times are a wonderful bonding experience! So be creative, be adventurous and make sure you take the time to plan some family fun. Use your organisational skills to get the good times happening – or they might not happen at all.

Every Sunday we play games together as a family, which is really fun.

Brad, 9

The current family fun is getting involved in shows (the girls are all currently on stage for *The Wizard of Oz*), but they have always enjoyed racing off to the park or the beach to play on the equipment and run around. The longer we can spend doing that the better.

Sonia, 30s

Love to me means closeness and doing things together and helping each other. My husband's parents recently built a deck. It was a grand occasion and it also marked the end of daylight saving. Grandparents, aunties, uncles and cousins were all there. We had a slap-up meal and we followed it up with a disco on the deck. We turned all the lights down low in the lounge and danced the night away with 70s music like Boney M and Abba. It was for the kids, but the adults loved it too!

Kerry, mid-30s

For my 40th birthday my husband organised a surprise party right under my nose. He invited family and friends and workmates. I thought I was going out to dinner and my parents who had travelled to stay would come too. A friend turned up to join us for a glass of wine beforehand when my nephew from Te Awamutu suddenly appeared at the front door saying, 'Happy Birthday, Aunty Di!' I looked past him down our front path and was astonished at what I saw. It seemed that coming down the path was everyone I knew! My mother said the look on my face was something to behold – the principal thing being, 'How am I supposed to feed everyone?'.

My daughters gleefully started pulling out potato chips, peanuts and other snacks from under their beds. Paper plates and plastic glasses tumbled out from their wardrobes, and salads and desserts appeared with every woman who came through the door. My husband started banging away and suddenly there was a bar over the spa pool on the back deck. A neighbour had been hoarding the booze! A girlfriend worked for a large catering outfit and brought along a hot baron of beef and pavlovas. Hey presto! We had a party going. It was a great night and a huge surprise to a person who thought they knew everything that was going on!

Dianne, 50s

We have had a lot of fun with family nights. We had Hawaiian nights where we had a picnic in the lounge (surrounded by pot plants) and 'Hawaiian music', and ate ham steaks with pineapple. We dressed up in holiday clothes: bright shirts and jandals. It was the middle of winter but good fun. Another time, when the boys were under 10, we had a dress-up night where they wore Dad's shirts and ties. I prepared a three-course meal, candles and printed menus. The food wasn't flash, but named with flair so it sounded exotic. We didn't go out much as a family so this was a treat for the boys – and a cheap night in. Another night I had six different menu items and a dice. Each person got to roll the dice once, and that number correlated to an item of food that we then ate. So it was a mixed-up meal – with ice cream before carrots, etc!

I enjoyed the creative aspect of family nights and the anticipation. Everyone in the house knew that family night was coming so the anticipation was a high component to its success. Having only boys can be tricky because they sometimes don't open up in their feelings, so doing fun things was important for me to find another way to communicate with them. Doing things together as a family adds a dimension to your life and makes you a unit. Anyone can live in a house, but the common purpose – common activity – helps bind you and gives you a culture. But I have never been strong on traditional family gatherings: I prefer to develop untraditional ways for our family times instead.

Heather, 42

Getting through the hard times

Without a family, man, alone in the world, trembles with the cold.

André Maurois

Difficult times strike us all. Job losses, money worries, ill health, the death of a loved one: life isn't always fair or just. But during times of adversity a person's family can be a place of refuge. Family can help care for you and provide an empathetic ear. A family feels with their own and provides a nurturing cocoon of comfort during times of trouble and sadness.

Last year when my grandmother had cancer I returned to the UK to be with her. The rest of the family is dotted around the world, yet they were always phoning and emailing her about how she was getting on. Mum and Dad even came out and joined us for a month, which meant the world to my grandma.

Jennifer, 21

I've found my daughters to be a great comfort in sad times. Just a hug or a 'What's wrong?' from them is a great energy boost for me. When my father died they all got to go and see him at hospital and then the funeral home, and we helped each other through by doing lots of talking and crying and laughing when we needed to.

Sonia, 30s

I have more to do with my extended whanau than I used to. I contacted one of the women and said I wanted to keep in contact with my roots, but I wanted to do it through the women. (My tribe is patriarchal and quite abusive and I didn't want to have much contact with the men, especially in regards to my children.) Primarily it was to share stories about how we got to where we are, about our children, that kind of thing. It worked a treat. Since then I have had so much more contact with them. It is all about honouring who we are as women. We have to acknowledge we are all great survivors. None of our lives have been easy. Most of the women have married hard men and have had really hard fathers. Several of them have abusive relationships. So to be able to step out of that is a wonderful thing. Instead of going 'poor me,' we can say instead, 'I made it. I am here now.'

Kiri, early 50s

My husband lost his job last year and was out of work for a few months. The children were wonderful. They rallied around him and said many things to encourage him; they also went out of their way to save money. I was so proud of the way they reacted.

Beth, mother of Jessica, 11, and Cody, 13

If I am upset, I tell my mum and she just sits with me and we talk about it. She finds a way to resolve the problem.

Lizzie, 10

Family love

Hugs and kisses

We need 4 hugs a day for survival.
We need 8 hugs a day for maintenance.
We need 12 hugs a day for growth.

Virginia Satir

All of us need to be hugged for our wellbeing. Children especially need physical touch and affection. In 19th-century orphanages more than half the infants died in their first year from 'marasmus', a Greek word meaning 'wasting away'. In the 1920s Dr Henry Chapin hired women to hold babies that had previously been in sterile wards but had seldom been picked up. Mortality rates dropped dramatically. Studies have shown that the toddlers with the most physical contact with their parents learn to walk and talk earlier. So get hugging!

Love is hugs and kisses.

Henry, 7

I love it when Mum reads me a book, but I love it best when I can sit on her lap when she reads. She kisses me lots and I like that too.

Annette, 8

Oh yes! Little kids give wonderful hugs!

Diana, grandmother of two little children

I am not sure what has worked to make my boys so comfortable with hugs and being physically demonstrative. I think they feel secure within the family. I was very conscious of ensuring that they developed their self-esteem and I read many books when I was pregnant. We believed children needed rules, not for the sake of rules, but to set boundaries. It is so essential in the first five years. That is a particularly busy time, because you can have a toddler and baby (or more) and it is so easy to give in and ignore behaviour that you don't want. I can still remember, even after two decades, the exhaustion I felt each evening after a day with pre-schoolers. I have always believed in discipline but I also equally believe in hugs. We had a story each night which was usually told curled up on the couch together. Some families have stories in bed but for us the couch was popular!

Neither of my boys went through the common stage of not hugging parents because it was 'uncool': coolness didn't matter in that way to them. My older boy would often sling his arm around me even if we were shopping, and was not self-conscious at all. He just didn't care what his mates thought. He is self-assured and confident in his own identity. He still enjoys teenage music, weird hairdos and stud bracelets, but those aren't important things to me – his own character and personality are what matters. How my boys treat and acknowledge others is what matters.

Heather, 42

Kind deeds

The little unremembered acts of kindness and love are the best parts of a person's life.

William Wordsworth

One of the easiest ways to show another family member that you love them is to do a kind deed. It could be as simple as taking the rubbish out when you know another family member really dislikes this job. It could be washing someone's car for them, doing the grocery shopping, or helping someone with their study or a hobby. These thoughtful acts of service gently heap up until they are a mountain of love.

On Sunday mornings I make my mum a coffee.

How-Shin, 9

My mum is an English teacher and she buys books for us if we are having trouble with a subject. She then sits down and helps us.

Jaimie, 10

My 14 year-old-son, Jacob, does a paper run once a week, which sometimes involves a lot of work for him. I was very impressed with Jacob's actions a while ago. After a couple of particularly busy weeks where we had worked quite hard, Jacob, on his own initiative, decided that he would take us out for breakfast as a way of saying thanks. Off we went to MacDonald's and Jacob proudly handed over his hard-earned money to pay for us all.

Catherine, 35

The girls like to make me breakfast in bed on special occasions. Sometimes it is a cup of tea and toast. Now that the eldest is a teenager and sleeps until after lunch she doesn't bother with that any more, but the other two like to try and make an effort. Usually I'm already up and racing off to do something or I'm so dead tired they try not to wake me. I think that's how they show they care – by letting me sleep in!

Sonia, 30s

My sister is the kindest person you could ever meet. Recently I had to go into hospital for an operation. She looked after my kids (along with her own) and did all my housework for the month it took me to recoup. She's amazing!

Fiona, 37

My sons came around last summer and painted my house for me. They said they were just going to do a bit of a tidy up around the property, but before I knew it they had painted the entire house. And a good job they did too! I have five sons and they often band together like this to get something done in life. They are good lads.

Jeremy, 82

My family is wonderful to me. My eldest son visits me every couple of days and helps me with the garden and maintenance around the house. My daughter takes me shopping every week and she recently bossed me into getting new glasses. My youngest son tries to improve my mind. He's always buying me books and taking me to see plays and movies. I know that they love me, not from what they say, but from what they do.

Evelyn, 71

Verbal appreciation

Words are, of course, the most powerful drug used by mankind.

Rudyard Kipling

Psychologists say that one of the deepest human needs is to feel appreciated. Simply telling someone in your family that you love them, or that you think they are special, that they did well in that rugby game or piano recital, or that you appreciate them paying the bills every month, is an easy way to show that you care. And often it is not just what you say that will make them feel loved, it is also the way you say it!

My family tells me that they love me and they are happy for me, or that they are concerned for me if there is a reason to be. They tell me they are proud of the person I am. I love their constant interest, support and encouragement of me and my life.

Sarah, 22

I know Mummy loves me. She says so all the time.

Melanie, 7

My mum always seems to know when I'm having a hard time. She'll put a note in with my lunch. The note is always on plain paper but the messages are always a bit OTT – 'Son, you are a unique person with a great personality', 'I'm proud of the way you don't give up on maths', that sort of thing – but it always makes me feel good about myself. It's choice!

Mitch, 16

My father uses a nickname for me that I have had since a baby. He calls me Lop Ear! It stems from me being a forceps baby and having one ear turned forward at birth. My grandchildren call me DeeDee – from the initial of my name. The use of these special names always makes me feel loved.

Dianne, 50s

When I was a lot younger I acted in my first play at school. My dad came along and said a whole heap of nice things afterwards. I felt really encouraged by him. Now I'm going to drama school. Thanks Dad!

Jasmine, 18

When I am in a sports game or competition, my mum and dad cheer for me!

How-Shin, 9

I was at a party the other night and I had several people come up to me to say what a wonderful mother I was. It seemed my husband had been talking about me when I wasn't around. That's kinda nice . . .

Maureen, mother of three

I've always dabbled in art, not thinking I was very good, until one of my children took me aside two years ago. He said to me, 'Mum, I'm not bullshitting, but you are really good at this art stuff. You should get serious.' Well, I'm still dabbling . . . but since his chat I have sold a few paintings and I have more confidence in what I am doing.

Joyce, 47

Quality time

Your family and your love must be cultivated like a garden. Time, effort and imagination must be summoned constantly to keep any relationship flourishing and growing.

Jim Rohn

With an increasingly busy lifestyle it can be difficult to find time to spend with your family. Between work and school, study and sport, and all the other activities squeezed into a day, family members end up passing each other on the stairs on their way out. Extended family members can live in the same town, but never find the time to see each other. One of the benefits of having quality time as a family is that it creates a memory bank, so it is worthwhile reviewing your schedules to find more time to spend together. Many studies have been done about TV viewing. Average figures say people watch between 15 and 21 hours of TV every week. Studies also show that children spend only 20 minutes a day in quality time with their mums, and only five minutes with their dads. Cutting back on TV could be the easiest way to create space for quality time in your family.

I like to hang out with my family. Sometimes we go to movies or theme parks. We play board games together. Often we just sit around and talk. My family is cool like that.

Jessica, 11

This is what I enjoy the most in our family. Every Sunday my sister comes around from her flat and my Uncle Ray and sometimes other family come along too. We just sit around and talk about the week. We do it every Sunday so it is like a ritual family thing.

Kate, 15

Our family plays sport – such as tennis, golf and swimming – together. We go for walks on the beach. We go out for lunches. We cook dinners for each other and share some wines in front of the fire. We go and visit relatives and have big chat catch-up sessions.

Sarah, 20s

We like to take long drives as a family to find new places of interest. We really love camping, which we do at least three times in the summer.

Mandy, 34

Everyone talks about quality time but I think any time is quality time. We are not huge TV buffs and we always have meals at the table together. I like starting the day together as it sets the tone for the day. At teatime, I used to ask the kids open-ended questions about their day, like, 'What was the funniest thing that happened today?' With teenagers, where possible we continue the tradition. It is harder because they are out and about more, but we still make the effort.

Heather, 42

Gift-giving

The manner of giving is worth more than the gift.

Pierre Corneille

Giving a small gift is one way to show someone in your family that you love them. And it doesn't matter if the gift doesn't cost any money: very often these are the best presents. A gift is a symbol that you have been thinking of the other person. From early years children enjoy giving presents to their parents, because gifts are a natural expression of love. Your gift can be purchased, found or made, and you don't need to wait until a birthday or Christmas to give a gift. A thoughtful impromptu gift is a beautiful expression of love. Gifts have nothing to do with monetary value. They have everything to do with love.

I love the simple things my grandchildren give me, like drawings they have done especially for Nan.

Diana, 58

My big bro gave me a Jonah Lomu book – and he stood in a queue for ages to get it signed, which was the best bit. My brother is awesome like that. He always buys me wicked gifts he knows I will like.

Hemi, 15

My favourite gift is a mirror with a beautiful carved wood surround. What I love most about it is that my son went to so much effort to get this mirror for me. He went into town in his wheelchair with his caregiver on a bitterly cold day and came all the way back with this big mirror on his lap.

Dianne, single mum of a 19-year-old who is paralysed from the chest down

Last birthday I got a teddy bear. It is my favourite gift because I can squeeze him when I'm not feeling good and it makes me feel better.

Amy, 8

My favourite gifts are a perfect heart-shaped stone my husband found on the beach, and a smiley-face ring my son bought me when he was young.

Josie, 40

The most precious gift I have been given is a tatty, old exercise book. Inside the scruffy exterior is the intermittent diary that my mother kept for the first few years of my life. Not only is this an amusing glimpse of myself as a baby and toddler, but it is a poignant look at my parents as a young married couple. Love, sheer love, pours from every page with my mother's reflections of the everyday moments in my family's life. My parents have since died, but thanks to this dishevelled diary, I have a window into my parents' lives when they were both vital and young, before illness and suffering.

Anne, mid-30s

Philia

FRIENDSHIP

If I don't have friends, then I ain't nothing.

Billie Holiday

Philia is the Greek word for the love between friends. The ancient Greeks considered friendship between men to be more important than marriage. In New Zealand today, men enjoy each other's company through shared activities, but would rather not vocalise thoughts about their friendships. Women, on the other hand, are generally happy to discuss these relationships and how they feel about each other. Studies show that people with good friends in their life feel less stressed, develop more self-confidence and can even live longer. Psychologists believe friendship is more important than it has ever been. Families today tend to be smaller, so people have less support from their immediate and extended family. Parents can be divorced, family members and relatives often don't live in the same town. Friendships are important! And friendships are the springboard to all other love. People with no friends often have difficulty in sustaining happy marriages or successful family relationships.

So try making new friends. Yes, some people find it easy to make friends and are easy to befriend. They are outgoing, talkative and have open spirits. But other people are shy and don't know how to reach out. Try building bridges. Choose people with good hearts. Compliment them, be kind and ask them open questions. Don't hide behind a mask – be honest, be yourself and let people discover the real you. And finally, be patient. Friendships take time to grow.

Nurture your old friends. And don't give up your friends if you get into a romantic relationship. No single person can meet all our needs. Old friends are one of the greatest blessings in life. We are fortunate indeed if we find that true friend who will share all the seasons of our life with us, who will be there to both grieve and celebrate with us. Friends like this may only come along once or twice in a lifetime.

Friendships can be as various as flowers in a garden. They may bloom once for a season, or they may slowly grow with pale colours deepening to strong hues over time. However long your friendship endures, cherish every moment, because friends help us move from merely living to being vibrantly alive!

New friends

The only way to have a friend is to be a friend.

Ralph Waldo Emerson

The origin of friendship can be unexpected and unpredictable. You could be room-mates at a conference. You could meet at the gym, on an aeroplane, at work or in a social setting. But there is something about this new person that you connect with and from that first contact a friendship can develop. Friendships are like plants and do wither away sometimes. People can develop other needs and interests and move away from the relationship. But don't be afraid to put energy into a new friendship. Celebrate a new friend and be grateful for the time you enjoy with them. And you never know: they could very well become old friends with time.

Without friendships you would be miserable. You would be sad and you would have no-one to love you.
Esther, 10

Friendships are important. If you didn't have any friends and you suddenly died, no-one would know about it.
Miller, 10

It is easy to make friendships. All you need to do is to be nice to other people and they will be nice back.
Caitlin, 12

You can touch someone's life, even if only for a few moments. I believe in the philosophy you can make a friend for an hour, sometimes. You could be sitting beside someone on an aeroplane, travelling together somewhere, just being friendly. You may never see them again but it doesn't matter. It is a nice experience. I know some people who are only interested in exploring old friendships or friendships they think have a future – but really who knows when friendships have a future? Sometimes they are just in the moment. They don't have to be forever.
Ian, 50s

Friendships for me mean accepting people and all their idiosyncratic ways. When you are younger you have high expectations but when you are older you just accept people and enjoy the differences. I find it easier to make new friends now because I am more tolerant of other people.
Mervyn, 57

I met a wonderful woman a few months ago at a barbecue. I liked her immediately and when we started talking we found we had a lot in common. When I was leaving I said to her that I thought we would become friends and she agreed with me. I have a feeling we are going to have a long and very beautiful friendship together.
Bernice, 35

Old friends

Old friends are best. King James used to call for his old shoes;
they were easiest for his feet.

John Selden

Old friends are a true blessing in a person's life. Together you have a shared history that serves to strengthen your friendship. Old friends are the ones that know you best. They have heard all your jokes a thousand times. They know the stories of how you broke your leg or the day you wrote off the company car or the day you celebrated getting your university degree. They know about your life – both the good and the bad – yet they still love you.

We met while we were both living in the nurses' home of the local hospital. She was a nurse and I was what they called back then 'a domestic'. I worked in the kitchen. She was the first person to cross the room to speak to me when the professionals and the domestics didn't mix. She smoothed the way for friendships between the two groups. We have now known each other 25 years.

What I most love about my friend is her acceptance of different cultures. She believes everybody should be treated the same. She doesn't judge people and she is loyal to friends. Our friendship is just always there. She's travelled overseas to live for a while and we've always written during these times. We have both had our ups and downs in life, but we have been there for each other. It is a supportive friendship. I feel so lucky to have had her friendship for so many years. Twenty-five years is a good chunk of one's life. She knows me warts and all, yet, despite that, we are the best of friends.

Joy, 42

There are some people that you meet that you just click with. I'm very comfortable with Philippa. We met when we were teenagers and we had only known each other a couple of years when I moved away. We nearly lost contact. I used to write all the time, but Philippa hardly ever wrote back. She's not much of a letter-writer, so I accepted that. Although she did write a letter to me once on a roll of toilet paper! It must have taken her hours. But I persevered and out of the blue she would ring me up every now and then. We have now been friends for 35 years. When we get together we just pick our friendship up where we left off. This is not something that has happened for me with many people.

Dale, 50s

I met my friend Wendy when our husbands had a business acquaintance. We have known each other now for 35 years. What I love most about Wendy is that she is a great listener and she is accepting of people, whether she agrees with them or not. She shows an unconditional love to family and friends and she has an enquiring mind, a sense of humour and understanding. We have a deep, caring friendship. We know we will be lifelong friends and that nothing will change that. Maybe we will end up in an old folks' home together!

Lilian, 72

Friends from a distance

About a month since I received and read Jane Eyre . . . After I read it
I went on to the top of Mount Victoria and looked for a ship to carry
a letter to you.

New Zealand settler Mary Taylor, in a letter to her friend Charlotte Brontë in England

Good friendships can endure separation. Even when a good friend lives overseas
there are still ways of keeping your friendship alive. The time-honoured written
letter is, of course, one option – but in a shrinking world with more technology at
our fingertips, phoning, emailing, faxing and text messages are all other options.
All it takes to be a friend to someone who lives elsewhere is a willing heart.

When I was living in Melbourne for over three years my friend always stayed in touch. She never stopped asking me when I was coming home! We missed being in the same town. We have now known each other for nearly 16 years and I love her unfailing loyalty, her encouragement and support.

Helen, mid-40s

I met Eleanor on the first day of primary school and I've known her for sixteen years. We moved to New Zealand when I was thirteen years old. It was very difficult for me as I found it hard to fit in with everyone at school. Eleanor always wrote to me during the first couple of years, supporting me with the changes that were happening. Now, after eight years away, we are still very good friends, although the writing has slowed down due to study. I send her texts or emails every now and then, even though we are on the opposite sides of the world. I'm there if she needs me. I know she cares too because she always shows an interest in what I'm doing and replies to any messages I send.

Jennifer, 21

I am very lucky to have three best friends who are three sisters. We have known each other for 20 years and we have a special friendship that never dulls. We can go years without seeing each other and months with no contact and whenever we get together it's like we have never been apart. Gerda is the oldest sister and she has exceptional taste and she is very generous. She is very arty and creative and her home looks like it could win awards. Helen is the middle sister who has always been my going-out friend: she is fun and lively and such a people magnet. Katherine is the career-orientated, switched-on, intelligent one. All in their own way make up one amazing friend. Helen is currently going through a terrible time – she was diagnosed with breast cancer and has just completed chemotherapy. I have never been homesick since I landed in New Zealand, but getting the news of her illness is the only thing that would pull me back to South Africa. I hope to get back to see her soon.

Mandy, 30s

Fun friendship times

Friends are the sunshine of life.

John Hay

Good times in life are even more fun when they are shared with a friend. You can be by yourself enjoying the most perfect of days but the true fun only really begins if a friend turns up to share it with you. And one of the most special aspects you can bring to a friendship is your humour. So lighten up, tell a joke, enjoy each other's eccentricities and take pleasure in the laughter.

My best friend makes everything so much fun. She has an amazing sense of humour and it doesn't matter what we are doing: sitting around drinking coffee, going for a walk, watching a video, she just always has me in fits.
Rachael, 25

When I visited my friend in Scotland last year we went to stay in a youth hostel and went clubbing in Glasgow for her birthday. Shopping is another pastime we have always shared and enjoyed – and this trip was no exception!
Jennifer, 21

I have a group of really wonderful friends. We always have a great time together. Everyone is quite creative, and a bit 'out there', so you never know quite what is going to happen at a dinner party or a barbecue. Invariably one of the men will end up dressing up in his wife's clothes for a laugh, or one of the girls will turn up wearing a pink wig or something – but it is all a heap of fun. I guess none of us has ever grown up – but we are having so much fun, why should we?
Cora, 47

What I enjoy most about my friendship with Brian is getting together for a game of squash and then going for a beer together afterwards. We really have a good time together. He is a great mate.
Shaun, 39

I love going on holiday with our closest friends that we have known for 20 years. We always have so much fun together. My husband and I have our own time, but we arrange to do·day trips and have dinner with our friends.
Marion, 52

Once a month I go to a friendship club. There are about ten women and I am the oldest. We are all grandmothers. We each take turns being the hostess for the day. We go out to a restaurant for lunch and then we go back to the hostess's house for a cup of tea. It is really nice and everyone is great. I really look forward to this each month!
Jean, 86

Getting through the hard times

We do not so much need the help of our friends as the confidence of their help in need.

Epicurus

When life deals you a bad hand of cards, there is nothing more special than a good friend who will partner you through the game. Hard times, tragedy and heartache are unfortunately part of the human existence at some time or another, but when times are tough a caring friend can make a considerable difference. They probably won't be able to change the situation, but just the fact they are there listening and supporting in a time of crisis means the burden is shared.

I'd just come out of an emotionally abusive relationship and was feeling very fragile. I was in tatters. After a long chat and admitting some home truths over a bottle of red wine we both ended up in tears. It made me feel so much better, though.

Carol, 20s

I had to attend a family group conference in Auckland that wasn't going to be pleasant, and my friend flew with me at her own cost to support me. She is always there for me.

Dianne, 36

I had just had the worst night of my life when I was out in town with my friends and this guy I was seeing. All my friends left and I ended up catching a cab home with my boyfriend and his ex-girlfriend – and my boyfriend wasn't coming home with me. I was so upset the only person I wanted to see was Rui, so at four in the morning I banged on her bedroom window, crying. She welcomed me, gave me her bed and made everything okay.

Sarah, 22

The day I left my last job was a distressing day. Odette was the first person I turned to. I arrived unannounced on her doorstep, having cried all the way there. She talked the whole thing out with me for hours. I love the way she encourages and supports me. She always makes time for me. And she makes good, helpful suggestions when things crop up in my life. Our friendship is non-judgmental, enduring, balanced and respectful.

Helen, early 40s

You can tell friends things you can't really tell your parents about. If you get in trouble at school you can't really tell your parents, but you can talk to your friends because maybe they are in trouble too.

Lizzie, 10

Thank you for being a friend

There is no wilderness like a life without friends; friendship multiplies blessings and minimises misfortunes; it is a unique remedy against adversity, and it soothes the soul.

Baltasar Gracian

Bronwyn shares how a caring friend helped her through the bad times.

I first met James through work. We lived in different cities but worked for the same company. We were both involved in sales and we spent six weeks each year travelling around New Zealand together. James is 20 years older than me and he always treated me with a great deal of respect. He was always the perfect gentleman. I was a little on the shy side but he slowly drew me out. James is very witty, highly intelligent and very caring of people. He's a true people person. After three years of working together I found that he was a person that I could really trust and despite the age gap we developed a strong friendship. We had a lot of interests in common and we had a very similar outlook on life. I also met James's wife, Angela, a few times and found her to be a really lovely woman whom I instantly liked.

   James changed jobs but we still kept in touch. He was always the friend I could phone up with a problem.

and ask for advice. He was always the friend that I could talk to about any issue without being concerned that he would be judgmental. I guess in a way he is part mentor, part big brother – and a little bit like a surrogate dad (my father died when I was young). I slowly got to know Angela over this time too. She is a woman I admire greatly. I feel doubly blessed to have two such wonderful people in my life.

After a few years I changed jobs and moved to the same city as James and Angela. It was a scary move as they were the only people I knew there. However, I was really excited about all the new opportunities in my life. I was busy with a new career, buying a house, making new friends and trying to put down roots in a new place. Unfortunately, everything went dramatically wrong. In a short space of time my mother died, I got very ill with glandular fever and I was attacked in my own home. I lost all my self-confidence. I've always been a happy, easy-going girl, but I completely lost my sense of self. I became severely depressed and even thought about suicide. I really thought I would never be happy again. Life was just a black void of endless, unrelenting despair. It is one thing to be physically hurt, but quite another to deal with the hurt of your soul, and I didn't know how to cope.

James and Angela stood by me during this time. I slept at their home for a time after being attacked, before I felt brave enough to go back home. When I went home we had a pact that I could phone them any time – day or night – and there were times that I did phone them in the wee hours. They never complained. The doctor put me on Prozac, but I felt ashamed about being on anti-depressants. I didn't want to go into the chemist to get the pills, so James would pick them up for me. James made me feel better when he told me that he too had had a period in his life when he had had to take some pills for a time. I went through a stage of feeling angry and smashing things. They just gave me space to talk about how I felt and helped me pick up the pieces of broken glass. I did a lot of stupid, irrational things during this time, but they never judged me; they just encouraged me to keep talking. I did go to a professional counsellor for a few sessions, but didn't like the experience at all. Maybe I just got the wrong person for me, but I found talking to people I trusted and knew already much more helpful. I am so fortunate that James and Angela were there to look after me.

It took time, but little by little I did heal. I did return to being the same happy, easygoing girl that I had been to begin with. I did regain 'myself'. I know having James and Angela as my friends helped me through this dark time.

Bronwyn, 32

Female friendships

I am treating you as my friend, asking you to share my present
minuses in the hope that I can ask you to share my future pluses.

Katherine Mansfield

Close female friendships can outlast boyfriends, can survive heartache and tragedy, and are the source of everlasting amusement and delight. Girls and women thrive on sharing their thoughts and feelings – and girl talk is an important element of female friendships. Honesty and acceptance are the key ingredients for a lifelong stew of friendship, liberally seasoned with laughter and fun.

Cath is fab. She is so honest. No matter what scraps I get into she's always there for me. She always finds something good to say. She always makes a huge effort to like my boyfriends, even if we both really know they are prats! Our friendship is solid. Nothing will ever break it up. She is the loveliest, kindest, funniest person I know. I'm not envious of her, but if I become a mother and I'm half as good as she is then I'll be delighted. Actually I'm very jealous of her hair – if you saw it you'd understand!

Carol, 20s

I met Rui at intermediate through classes, and also because we participated in netball and water polo and the Maori club. We've known each other 12 years and I love the fact that she will never be judgmental towards me. I can tell her the ugliest truth about myself and know that she won't hold it against me. Friendships are so important. It is easy to let them fade when you leave school and get partners and jobs, but you need to put in the effort to maintain them because you never know when someone will need you or you may need them.

Sarah, 22

Claire and I met at intermediate when we were 10 years old, but it wasn't until high school that we got to know each other and became friends. Our relationship is close, protective, nurturing, creative and a lot of fun. I remember getting lost in the wetlands near Whatipu and wading into deeper and deeper water, then getting uncontrollable giggles as water poured into the tops of our gumboots. And performing a 'skit' in which I read a poem about trees while Claire projected her photographs of trees onto me. And there have been endless cups of tea and glasses of wine as we've solved each other's problems for the last 20 years.

Jane, 35

We have been friends for 17 years. We first met when we worked together at a supermarket after school. I think the fact we are dissimilar is good because we see things differently and we get a diverse angle on things. Vanessa is even and sensible, while I'm a bit wacky and outgoing. I mellow her out and she keeps me on the straight and narrow.

Kerry, 30s

Male friendships

Think where man's glory most begins and ends
And I say my glory was I had such friends.

William Butler Yeats

Male friendships are often formed around shared activities and common experiences. All around Godzone male bonding occurs in the workplace, around the computer, on the rugby field, in the armed forces, or over a beer after work. And a good mate is a boon in life.

I've got two best friends and they both have really good senses of humour. They both like the same kind of things as me: the same sort of computer games and the same toys.

Joshua, 10

I met Rupert two years ago at school. He was a good friend of my girlfriend at the time and our friendship grew from there. He hangs out with me and is there for me if I ever need help. He is in a band and he lets me go along with him to all the shows he plays at. He is a very close friend and he is like a brother to me. I'm not ashamed to say it, but I love him – in a friendship kind of way though!

Chris, 18

I met my mate Owen when I was 18. I knew him for a couple of years and then he went to Vietnam. We used to write letters and when he came back home he used to come and see me and my wife. He would come up every Friday and he wouldn't leave until he had drunk every bottle in the house. I still have a lot of contact with him. We just have a connection. I can ring him up any time and have a yabber to him. We go out and it will be a great night. We can be in each other's company for bloody hours and not have to say much. He's a special person in my life and always will be.

Don, early 50s

The relationships between men in Godzone are often more appropriate to the early colonial times in our country than they are to the present. 'Bloke-ism' became a normal existence when the number of men in the country far exceeded the available women and large numbers of men lived in all-male communities. Many of them were rough communities: bush camps, mines, railway gangs, shearers, farmers and so on. Strong bonds of 'mateship' were formed and this kind of staunchness is still encouraged in such environments as the defence forces, police, fire, search and rescue and the like.

If you have been a member of a 'tooth arm' or fighting unit, the guys (and now women too) that were in your unit will have been closer to you than your family. Every member of that unit has to be able to trust every other person to do their job – at all times. I'm an ex-infantryman from NZ V-Force. I don't belong to any of the veterans' organisations, but I keep in contact with a few of the blokes. Despite the little contact I have with other vets, if any of the blokes I served with sent out a mayday call, I would be there, and so would the others. It is a bond that just doesn't go away. You can observe this kind of intense mateship in all sorts of places although it may not be as intense in, say, a sports team, as it will be in a bush gang – the element of shared risk seems to intensify the bond.

Bruce, 56

Friends for more than 60 years

No man is the whole of himself. His friends are the rest of him.
Proverb

Bob, a pilot in World War Two, talks about the long friendship he has had with two of his crew.

I first met Ian and Geoffrey on an RAF station in England. It was early 1944. We went through our training flying various aircraft. When we got to the bigger aircraft I got to pick a crew of six. They put us all together and they said to the pilots that we had a couple of hours to pick our crew. An evil-looking mob they were too! There were air gunners, wireless operators, bombers and navigators. They were all looking at us and we were all looking at them. I thought I'd get a Kiwi navigator if I could, so I spotted Geoffrey standing across the way. I approached him and asked if he would like to join my crew. He said, 'Yeah, okay.' So then the two of us had a look around for a Kiwi bomb aimer and a Kiwi wireless operator. The other three boys were English. That is how we got together.

There is something about those years. If you weren't over there at that time you wouldn't quite understand. There was a different atmosphere. It was war. We sensed that as soon as the ship pulled into Liverpool. All around there were barrage balloons to keep the German dive-bombers up high when they attacked. If the Germans flew low they would crash into the wires that tethered the balloons. There were anti-aircraft guns everywhere. It was a grey cold day in November and I had a look around. Boy, this was for real!

By the time we started to do operations in 1944, the really tough part of the war was over, so we were lucky. As an air force crew we relied on each other to a large extent. As the navigator, Geoff had to do his job to get us there. When we got there Ian had to do his job to drop the bombs. I managed to get them into the air and get them back out again. When we came back after an operation we would have a debriefing and we would have to say what the weather was like in Germany, what their anti-aircraft fire was like, if we had seen any German night fighters, and all that sort of thing. We were usually very tired. It was a seven- to nine-hour trip. But there was always coffee, usually with a good solid jolt of rum. It made a bloke want to queue again to get into the debriefing!

We were young, fit guys, and it was an adventure. We wouldn't have missed it for the world. It was a wonderful experience, particularly for me because I loved flying. Fortunately we had a crew that got on well together because it wasn't always the case. We did a lot of things together as a crew and we had a bond.

Geoff has a great sense of humour. He is a really good bloke, old Geoffrey. Ian also has a great sense of humour and he's very likeable. We have an awful lot of fun laughing.

During the war we had an old car that we bought for 10 pounds. We used to get round in this decrepit old car, myself and Ian and Geoff. It was a Jowett and had a hood that folded down. We would go tootling down these country lanes with the hood down, happy as Larry, going to some pub or other.

We had a friendship with a local farmer. He had a tractor and he got special fuel rations for his tractor. So we had an agreement about the petrol. We often had about half a dozen fresh eggs in the back of the car too. In those days a fresh egg in England was worth its weight in gold. All you got normally was powdered eggs. Ian was very good at going out and getting friendly with the local farmers, and he picked up quite a lot of eggs. One day we arrived at our destination with six or seven dozen eggs. You should have seen the women's faces when we turned up with these. We were quite popular at that stage!

After the war a lot of blokes were very unsettled when they came back to New Zealand. Some of them had done quite well and had had good promotions. Then all of a sudden it was over. I found it humdrum coming back to New Zealand and it wasn't easy at the time. You gradually settle down and get back into things, but it takes a while. Ian felt the same way. Geoff went back into the service. He married an English girl and I was the best man at their wedding. She couldn't settle in New Zealand so they went back to England. When he got over there he rejoined the RAF for 22 years. We kept in touch by writing letters and we saw each other whenever Geoff visited New Zealand. After his wife died, Geoff came back to New Zealand. He lives in the Hawke's Bay and we often talk on the phone. We are in regular contact and he's a great friend.

Ian and I have lunch together every couple of weeks. I was widowed four years ago. Ian was widowed this year. They had been married about 60 years those two; it was very sad. Ian and I are very close. My son Ian was named after my friend Ian, and Ian named his boy Bob after me. Poor unfortunate child! Although he has turned out really well.

Geoff is an ex-Kings College boarder and they asked him to give the address at an Anzac Day service a couple of years ago. He is a well-travelled serviceman but he said he wanted us to go and support him. So we went along, he called us up to the dais and introduced us. It was a nice day and it was good to be able to support Geoff. The three of us support each other a lot.

When we are together the 60 years just melt. We are the only people we can talk to about the war days. We are the only people that understand those days. What the atmosphere was like over there and all the friends we made. We just can't talk to anyone else about it. That is all there is to it. Ian and Geoff are good chaps; they are great mates.

Bob, 83

Showing you care

Verbal affirmation

If I had one gift that I could give you, my friend, it would be the ability to
see yourself as others see you, because only then would you know how
extremely special you are.

B.A. Billingsly

Sincere compliments for no other reason than to make someone else feel good are
the icing on the cake of life. Dare to talk about your affection. Be bold and tell
your friend what you like about them. Be cautious with criticism; instead encourage
and support your friends in their lives. To be the friend who inspires another to
move forward more confidently in life is a beautiful act of love.

My best friend just seems to know when to ring and say something encouraging. It's almost telepathic.

Susie, 27

Vanessa my friend often says that I am a good mum and that it comes naturally to me. That makes me feel like I am doing things right.

Kerry, 30s

When I got my new job I was nervous about moving to a new town and away from family and friends. My friend always pointed out the positives and made me feel capable by telling me I would be fine.

Sarah, 22

I met Monty about five years ago when I worked on *Shortland Street*, the TV show. He is an extraordinarily talented photographer. He is an amazing friend and he has encouraged me to do magazine styling. When we work together he always tells me I did a good job. I got a large shoot with 22 people to style recently. I said I couldn't do it. Monty said, 'Yes, you can.' It often takes someone else to believe in you for you to do things. So I did the styling and afterwards everyone told me how good it was. It all just fell into place beautifully.

Sonia, early 30s

Claire encourages me all the time. I don't think she has ever said a negative thing to me and won't let me say negative things about myself. My creative side is something I'm always letting 'lapse' and Claire is always encouraging me to take on new projects. She seems to believe I can do anything. Her faith in me is one of the great things in our friendship.

Jane, 35

Quality time

We can do what we wanna
Cos today the world is ours
Nothing gray, just real time and colours
In which to whittle away the hours.

Brooke Fraser

The gift of time is one of the most loving things you can give a friend. Simply hanging out together, enjoying each other's company and creating an opportunity to talk are among the greatest pleasures in life. It is almost incidental what you do during your time together. It is all about nurturing your friendship.

I have a group of friends rather than one best friend. My friends are just fun. You can go out and be yourself. They are not judgmental, they are laid-back and you don't have to worry about what will happen the next day about something you have said. We meet often and just sit around and talk for hours. We just hang out.

Kate, 15

Charles and I enjoy a game of golf together once a week. We enjoy the game, but I think what is more important is that we get time to talk.

Ron, 53

My friend always makes such an effort to be with me on my birthday, no matter where I am in New Zealand. She'll come and hang out with me and I appreciate that so much. We like to do adventurous things together – like we went sky-diving. We also like to vege out together with lots of yummy food and videos and just relax and chat.

Sarah, 22

The thing I like best about my friend is that we can laugh together. We have heaps of fun without doing a huge amount of things. It could be just listening to music and reading books, or going on a sightseeing trip around Christchurch. Sometimes he plays the piano and I just enjoy listening. It's just the time together that is good.

Marian, 21

We do yoga together every week and often have a meal together afterwards. It's a chance to catch up and just be together. We do a lot of socialising together so it's not necessary to consciously take time out for each other. But on the rare occasion when I don't see her during the week it always feels like we've been apart for AGES. We've been on trips together, just the two of us, and it always works out really well as we have a similar appreciation for nature and the same ideas of what we want out of a trip.

Jane, 35

We have lunch every Monday to catch up on the weekend and take time out of the office. We plan dinners together and we have girly nights watching silly DVDs. I know that Carolyn and I will have a life-long friendship even when we no longer work together. Her daughters and my son are friends and our husbands are also great mates. I feel really blessed to have met her.

Josie, 40

Kind deeds

We cannot tell the precise moment when friendship is formed. As in filling a vessel drop by drop, there is at last a drop which makes it run over. So in a series of kindnesses there is, at last, one which makes the heart run over.

James Boswell

Friendships are all about thoughtfulness – and as with watering a plant, it is kind deeds that allow a relationship to grow. Often it is the small everyday things that really show you care. It could be helping a friend study or it could be sharing something you own. It could be cooking a meal and inviting your friends over. It could be organising a working bee at a friend's property to help them fix up their garden. The thoughtful acts you can do for a friend are without end!

When I was at the hospital with my son, my friend cleaned the whole of my house so I didn't have to do a thing when I got home.

Dianne, 30s

My best friend is an awesome cook. I'm the opposite. I just don't have the know-how in the kitchen. She invites me over for dinner once or twice a week and cooks the choicest food. She says it's nothing, but I'm stoked by her kindness. I try to find other things I can do for her in return.

Waipuni, 20s

I'm studying at university and I've really been struggling with one of my papers – a chemistry one. It just hasn't been gelling for me. Fortunately one of my friends is a real brain-box in this area. He's so good to me. He's been coming over to my place for the last few weeks to help me study.

Katherine, 19

Some of the boys got together and they came around and rebuilt a fence that was wrecked in a storm. They are wonderful friends to us.

Mairi, 43

We are shameless promoters of each other. I have often found myself having to give impromptu poetry readings as Claire has been telling someone how good my poetry is. This faith and enthusiasm for me and my projects always makes me feel appreciated.

Jane, 30s

We have been doing house renovations and I've been showering at my friend's place now for five months. They never make me feel uncomfortable about this. I'm really grateful to have a friendship like this. When you don't have family close by it is really important to have friends that genuinely care about you.

Sonia, early 30s

Physical closeness

A hug is the shortest distance between friends.

Fridge magnet

Admittedly New Zealanders tend to be reserved when compared with people from some other countries. But especially in times of crisis or in times of great excitement, a simple hug or a pat on the back is a wonderful way to show your friends that you care. Sometimes non-verbal communication can be more powerful than all the words of a dictionary.

In our circle of friends we were never much for hugging when we were young, but as we have got older I find that we are all much more comfortable with this. Now it would be strange if we didn't greet each other with a hug.

Gladys, 62

I wouldn't say that I'm that physically demonstrative around my friends, but I do like to shake their hands or give them a pat on the back if they have good news and something to celebrate.

Paul, 35

My friend and I are not really physically demonstrative but we're physically very comfortable together. I think this is because we have been friends since we were teenagers and hugging and kissing friends then was very uncool. So that's the behaviour we are used to. As adults you don't decide one day, 'OK, let's start hugging each other when we meet now.'

Jane, 35

I know this will sound a bit unusual, but there are a group of us who love having our feet scratched. Occasionally we end up sitting in a circle scratching each other's feet. It is wonderful that we are comfortable enough as friends to do this. It feels wonderful!

Joana, 55

My very best friend was terminally ill for some months before she passed away. I moved into her home to help care for her, along with support from her children who visited daily. We had never been particularly demonstrative in all the years we were friends, but during her last months I was constantly hugging her, stroking her hand, rubbing her back. The hospice nurses told me that touch is very important to people when they are ill, and I found it was a very natural expression of my love for her as a friend in those final months. It was a simple way to bring her comfort and to show that I cared. I miss her greatly, but the last months of her life were a very special time. It was a very sad time, but also a time of great love with no barriers up.

Geraldine, 59

Gift-giving

Giving presents is a talent; to know what a person wants, to know when and how to get it, to give it lovingly and well.

Pamela Glenconner

Small, thoughtful gifts are a lovely way to show a friend that you care about them. And any day is a good day to give a friend a gift: you don't need to wait until their birthday or some other special occasion. A gift is a way to show that you have been thinking of them. It has nothing to do with the money spent, but all to do with the sentiment behind the giving.

My friend gives me thoughtful gifts of the moment: fruit from the orchard; a book; a pot of jam.

Lilian, 72

I really love a greeting card that my friend sent when I'd moved into a flat. It made me feel special when I was having a really rough time.

Carol, 20s

My best friend will often pop around with flowers and a bottle of wine. She is incredibly generous and thoughtful.

Michele, 40s

My favourite gift is a lovely gold and sapphire ring that my three best friends gave to me on my 21st birthday. They know exactly what I like and I wear it always.

Mandy, 34

My friend knew Mother's Day was going to be difficult for me as I had had two miscarriages and my mother's cancer had recently returned. She gave me a lovely bread-making book out of the blue. I love cooking and this thoughtful gift really helped me to focus on something nice during a sad time for me.

Joy, 42

My best friend gave me the coolest gift. It is a framed photo of the two of us. On the matte part inside the frame she wrote in metallic pen some friendship quotes and some things about what our relationship means to her.

Amelia, 17

My best friend and I celebrate a friendship day once a year. We always exchange a little gift. I'm a big kid at heart and love soft toys, so she always gives me a teddy bear. She's a bookworm so I always get her a nice hardback. After 22 years we both have a beautiful collection of gifts that are a wonderful reminder of our enduring friendship.

Samantha, 39

Agape

LOVE OF HUMANITY

You will find as you look back upon your life that the moments when you have truly lived are the moments when you have done things in the spirit of love.

Henry Drummond

Agápe is the divine love from God to humankind and from humanity to God. It is also the love and benevolence that occurs throughout the human race when people choose to care for others.

Agápe is the most common form of love in the Bible. It is the love that motivates someone to save the helpless and assist the less fortunate. It is the love that drives people to help even their enemies. Agápe love focuses on how someone can meet another person's needs. It is the most selfless of all the loves – and it is the love that we most need in the world today.

The world is full of caring, generous, loving people. Everywhere there are invisible armies of compassionate people who show agápe to other people each and every day. They are our quiet heroes who are seldom credited for the loving deeds they perform. Some do everyday acts of kindness for people that they come in contact with. They help their arthritic neighbour by mowing their lawns for them. They baby-sit for the solo mum across the road so she can study. They visit a lonely elderly man several times a week and keep an eye on him. Other people volunteer or are employed by a variety of different organisations that are helping people around the country.

If you open up the first few pages in your local telephone directory you will see a list that shows some of the love, care and compassion that happen in our communities: Age Concern; counselling services; city missions; budget advice;

help lines. These organisations are only some of countless groups making our nation a better place to live in. And other people are working around the world in some of the worst trouble spots, helping war-ravaged and poverty-stricken nations rebuild.

Giving your expertise, time, energy or money to help other people is a wonderful thing. It creates ever-expanding circles of caring that can change the world in a positive way. Individuals can make a difference in others' lives. And individuals working together with love in their hearts for a common good are an even more powerful force: they have the ability to transform the world.

Agápe, the God-like love of humanity, is the most generous, astonishing, wonderful love of all.

Caring for others

Something that rises
beneath the curved
ribs, catching the
updraft of vision.
Unending kite
on the string
of love.

Bob Orr

It is a selfless, God-like love that inspires someone to help the needy, feed the hungry or be a listening ear. Every person who cares for someone else in the community helps make the world a better place. We are not helpless in the face of violence, poverty, hopelessness, illness or addiction. Even as individuals we can make a difference and if individuals band together the results can be startling.

If I did a good deed for 10 people, and they did good deeds for other people, then one person can make a difference. You just need to be able to stand up for yourself. You have to have the confidence to do something.
Jaimie, 10

It is important to do things for other people because some people can't do things for themselves and they need help. And if you help others you also feel good about yourself. You don't feel all mean and selfish. And sometimes you gain more friends.
Lizzie, 10

I reckon different people have different qualities so what you do is you get lots of people and then as a group you can do things together to help others.
Esther, 10

Helping other people is all about respect. And if you respect someone then you will get respect right back.
Tane, 9

It is easy to care for your partner, your family and your friends — what sort of person would you be if you didn't? But it is a special person who steps out their front door and seeks out others to care for. I know my wife goes out of her way to visit an elderly neighbour for a cup of tea and a chat on a regular basis because she knows this lady is lonely. That's the sort of thing I'm talking about. It is only a small example but New Zealand needs more of this sort of caring.
Max, 42

The act of giving freely to, and caring for, others is the lubricant of our society. It is the stuff that dissolves fear and aggression and makes people act towards others positively. I call it altruism. It is one of the hardest things in the world to do.
Terry, 50s

Making a difference in an older person's life

I am only one, but I am one. I cannot do everything, but I can do something.

Edward Everett Hale

A volunteer for Age Concern for more than ten years talks about his work and how people can make a difference in the world, one person at a time.

I have a love of humanity, a feeling that just overtakes me sometimes. It comes in a gush. I don't know where this feeling comes from, but occasionally I just like everybody for no particular reason. It isn't something I can put my finger on.

I believe you can make a difference in the world. If you can touch one person, if you can do something good for them, that can make a difference. It doesn't have to be a crusade. If everyone did something nice for one person every day just imagine how that would multiply and the difference it would make — and then that would empower those people to go on and do something nice for someone else also. It would be a never-ending, expanding situation.

I wanted to do something. I wanted to put something back, but I was uncertain of what to do. I was talking to a friend of ours who is a nurse and she came up with the suggestion of volunteering for Age Concern. I thought, why not? My parents were quite a lot older when I was born and I'm used to dealing with older people and I have always got on well with them. It was something I felt I could do: it was a good fit.

My work for Age Concern involved me being an advocate for one particular person. You could be an advocate for more than one if you wished, but due to work and other things there is only so much you can do. And it goes back to the philosophy of just taking on one project and doing it properly. So I had someone assigned to me that I visited. I was there to look out for them. Normally I would visit Betty once a week for an hour or two and I would keep in touch by phone during the week. My role was to be her confidante and support person.

Age Concern gave us training about elderly people. What really gave me a buzz was the number of people on my training course and the different backgrounds they came from. There were some people there that were as young as 20 and some who were older than the people they were visiting! There were a wide range of people from psychiatrists, tradespeople to salespeople – all sorts of people. They just wanted to do something. And I think that is a good cross-section of people in life anonymously helping others. It doesn't make headlines, but there are a lot of people quietly doing good things out there.

I know my visits did make a difference. Sometimes when Betty was feeling depressed, by the end of the visit she would be quite happy and hearty. Sometimes she would be cheered up before I got there. I was able to, at least for a short period of time, make her feel a little more stimulated and we had some fun.

I visited Betty for more than 10 years. It is a huge commitment. You can't take it on and then get tired of it in two or three years' time, get too busy and walk away from it, because people form relationships with you and they have expectations of you. You have to keep going.

It was enjoyable sometimes and other times it wasn't so much. If you enjoy it, it is a bonus. You are there to help people, and helping people isn't always going to be enjoyable. It might sound fantastic, but people are people and they can get grumpy and they have their ups and downs. Your role is to provide some sort of mental stimulation for them.

I think it is important for people to do volunteer work in the community and I know a lot of people that do. I think you would be surprised how many people do informal volunteer work. The formal thing is when you work for an organisation like Age Concern. It is almost like a dating service. You want to do a good deed, but you don't know how to find someone that needs you to do it for them, therefore they match you up. And there are a lot of organisations like that around.

It's all about giving back. I have had my ups and downs but I've had a very good life and I think that is an appreciation of having a good life, doing some little things for someone else. I haven't had a lot of drama and difficulties, and when you come from that sort of privileged position in life, you probably owe it to society, and even to God, to put something back.

Ian, 56

Caring for the terminally ill and dying

If we have been pleased with life,
we should not be displeased with death,
since it comes from the hand
of the same master.

Michelangelo

Hospices throughout New Zealand are doing the special job of caring for the terminally ill and the dying. Doctors, nurses and volunteers work together to help relieve pain and suffering; they provide emotional and spiritual support; and they do their utmost to make every day the best day possible for terminally ill patients and their families. The result is that terminally ill patients have dignity and respect as they approach the unavoidable journey through death.

I was interested in working for the hospice, so I went along to an introductory course. We covered human psychology and caring for the dying. Interestingly, the hospice training is not so much concentrated on dying – it's focussed on making the best of life and living for those who are terminally ill. A key part of my role is just to be there, in virtually every case to release the primary caregiver who, by the time we come on the scene, has already gone through a lot. People tend to be very honest when they are terminally ill and conversations can be quite deep at times. You often get insights into other people's lives that enhance one's understanding of human nature and the bonds we share.

David, 70s, hospice homecare volunteer

I get a lot of satisfaction from my work. We do a lot of empowering for the patient and their families. I often meet people who are very apprehensive about what hospice is and what we are going to do. They fear what's going to happen in the future and how they are going to manage. But just by being there and giving them support I find it's very rewarding to see how families and patients do cope with what's happening to them.

When we are in the home we focus totally on the patients and their families. Sometimes we just sit and listen. Other times we deal with their symptom control. We monitor any pain or nausea, making them comfortable, and we'll address any other symptoms that may be concerning them. I'm always aware that we are there as guests at their invitation. It is a real privilege to care for someone who is dying and to go into their home.

Jan, 40s, hospice nurse

The kitchen is the hub of the hospice unit, where the food is prepared, but more importantly where people can come and talk. Our kitchen is accessible to all the families and we find, especially after 5 p.m., people come into the kitchen and often want to talk to someone who is one step removed from the nurses. And there we are working with pots and pans, representing some sort of normality. Just like at home where often the best conversations happen in the kitchen, people come and make a cup of tea and 20 minutes later they are still there talking.

Gisela, 50s, housekeeper at hospice

There are about 20 women on the Fundraising Events Committee, although I'm trying to encourage men to join. We break into sub-committees for the different events we organise. I'm one of those people who like to give – but from that you receive a lot. Volunteering for the hospice is something I really love. There is also a wonderful group of ladies on the committee and lovely friendships have come out of that. So that is a real bonus. And I know that the work we do is fundamental in keeping the hospice going. The work the hospice does blows me away. The staff and volunteers at hospice are a damn good team.

Therese, 30s, volunteer fundraiser for hospice

Loving our young people

Live your beliefs and you can turn the world around.

Henry David Thoreau

Compassionate and caring, Dave and Penny are a married couple with a genuine love for young people. For the last 12 years they have worked at a student youth hostel, more often than not becoming surrogate parents to their young charges.

DAVE: The youth hostel is one of the Baptist Action agencies. The prime reason for the hostel is to provide a Christian home for New Zealand students outside of Auckland who are coming here for the first time and going to university. We also take some overseas students. We look after up to 35 young people aged 17 and 18.

The students have to apply to come here and there is an interview process that they go through. We offer full board and they don't have to bring anything from home. There is breakfast every morning, they can make their own lunches, and there is a nice evening meal at 6 p.m.

We get the full spectrum of students from extroverts to the very quiet withdrawn ones. Sometimes we get students who need a lot of extra love and attention. Some of them come from very disturbed families and they are trying to do something better for themselves.

We have been doing this since 1992. We came along as assistants to help and we have been here ever since! At first I was working full time as well as working here. We lived upstairs in a one-bedroom flat, just a tiny room, for the first three years. I used to leave to go to work at 7 a.m., come back at 4.30 p.m., and start doing my work here at the hostel at 5 p.m. and work through to 10 p.m. Penny worked full time in the hostel during this time.

PENNY: We consider this work a mission rather than a job. I hope we are making a small difference in these young people's lives. I like seeing them when they are ready to go into the world. It is nice to know we have been a little part of their lives to help them on their way.

I said to the students this morning, 'I don't know what I'm doing here because I really don't like young people', and of course, they all roared with laughter! You couldn't do this job if you didn't love young people.

We have to turn a blind eye to some of the pranks that happen. Young people will be young people! You can't be dictatorial: it doesn't work. They still have to have rules and know their boundaries but they are not children.

Some of the boys were locked out of their rooms last night. It was the girls' pay-back time for what the boys did to them. Some of them slept in the lounge. So I said to them, 'Did you have a good sleep?' And they said, 'Oh, you heard.' I just look at them and think when I was that age I used to get up to those sorts of things too. I have a laugh with them.

Often all they need is a hug and I'm a hugger so that works out well.

DAVE: Some 17-year-olds are children while other 17-year-olds are very mature, so you have to weigh this up. They are young people and they get up to all the tricks in the book, but as long as there is no damage we are fine with it. They should enjoy living in a hostel. They should have fun and we encourage them to take part in the hostel activities.

Recently we played 'angels and mortals'. I put all the students' names into a hat, and I pulled out each of their names and that person became another person's 'mortal'. The 'angels' had to do nice things for their mortals for a week. It could be buying them a bar of chocolate; writing a verse; anything creative and nice. Most of our young people are creative, so they came up with all sorts of ideas. And then after a week we had a session revealing who everyone's angel was. It brings them all together and is good fun.

We have devotional readings each night. It is surprising how often they all sit looking at you without saying anything and then a couple of days later they will come up and talk to you and you will find it has really affected that person. And even if you only touch one person and get them thinking about deeper issues, it is worth it.

That is one problem with society these days: there are lots of people with qualifications but they don't know how to handle life. Hopefully, we teach them a bit of life here. All the students in the hostel are going to make something of themselves. It is really encouraging for us to see previous students go on in life. We have doctors, a missionary over in northern Pakistan, and a young woman who is in Cambodia looking after prostitutes there. She saw her father shot, escaped the Khmer Rouge and ended up in a camp. She was here at our hostel for two years and now she is working to help others.

I've been thinking about why we do this work. It has been a gradual process and we didn't set out to do this. But God gives you gifts. We have been doing this for 12 years now and we really enjoy what we do.

The students often go flatting nearby because they want to be near the university and we often get invited out to dinner. When you get invites like this you think you must have done something right. It makes it worth it. And hopefully that is how it works: you make a difference in their lives and they go on to make a difference.

We build up a strong bond with these kids and that is what it is all about. For this job you have to have your health (you couldn't do it if you didn't), you have to have the desire, and you have to have the love for the kids.

Penny and Dave, 50s

Everyday acts of kindness

You must be the change you wish to see in the world.
Gandhi

Kiwis are generous, caring people in the main. There are many things that people do each and every day to help others in some way or another. Together all these small acts of kindness create a community of caring, all helping specific individuals and making the world a much nicer place to live in.

If you go to the supermarket there are these boxes that you can put food in for charity. Our family does that.

Samantha, 9

We support a child through World Vision.

Matt, 11

When I was having chemotherapy two of my teenage son's friends wrote to me during this difficult time. They blew me away. Louise wrote me letters that were addressed to 'Dearest Angel Ainslie' and her letters were chatty and breezy. She included photos so I could see what was going on in her life. Her letters were just rays of sunshine. Mitchell wrote me handwritten letters. They were very deep and were pages long. The two of them also sent cards and gifts. The parents knew what they were doing but never knew what they were writing. I just cannot say how special they were to write to me like this. They kept it up the whole year and I've kept every one of their letters.

Ainslie, 40s

We decided as a family to have a Christmas tin. We all put in what we would have spent on presents for each other and just before Christmas we have special time, with hot chocolate and marshmallows, and we count the money and decide who will be the recipient.

We always try to choose a charity or missionary that we don't know much about. Then we bank the money and write a cheque and send it to the recipient. We have had lovely letters back from them expressing their delight at our new tradition.

With our new way of giving at Christmas it takes huge pressure off all of us at a time of year when shopping goes crazy. Even some of our relatives have joined in and instead of sending a present to us they donate to a charity. Last year friends donated money to an African project for a goat and relatives donated to the same charity – for a heifer! That was great for us because we do not need presents and someone else benefits.

Heather, 42

Fostering a child

Blessed is the influence of one true, loving human soul on another.

George Eliot

A young couple talks about the rewards and challenges of being foster parents to a five-year-old girl.

RYAN: We didn't think we would be able to have children. We thought about adopting a baby but that didn't work out. Then some friends of ours were fostering this little girl, Amber. Our friends work full time and all their children are adults. They thought Amber should be with people who were younger. So we knew this little girl needed a home and we made enquiries about fostering her.

RACHEL: Amber got placed in another home but it didn't work out. I was quite blue to find out it hadn't worked. I was really disappointed for her. So then she went back to our friends' place, and we got a phone call asking us if we were still interested in fostering her.

RYAN: I had sat down with Rachel and said we had to give up on the idea of having children. We weren't going to have kids, but it wasn't the end of the world. There were other things we could do. We could travel. I had an idea about selling the house and buying a bus and travelling around America because we would have the freedom to do it. Then I got a phone call at work in June and I was told that Amber needed a home. I said 'Yes' to fostering her. They phoned Rachel independently and she said the same thing. We never sat down and discussed it at that stage, but we both said 'Yes'.

The department rang us in November and said Amber would come to our place after Christmas. She was staying with our friends and she was going to spend Christmas with her family. So we arranged to go to their place on Boxing Day and we spent a few days with Amber before we brought her back with us. Five days later I was working on a roof when Rachel rang to say she was pregnant. I sat on the roof for an hour. In the space of a week we had gone from no children to two children. Amber is five and we have been looking after her for 19 months now.

The department thought Amber needed to go where she would be an only child, where she would get absolute attention and devotion. They thought we sounded like a couple that could do that. Right at the last moment we threw a spanner in the works with the news that Rachel was pregnant, but thankfully they changed their minds about Amber being an only child. They thought if she grew up with a baby she might actually see how life should have been for her right at the start.

RACHEL: Amber is starting to form a bond with the two of us. These kids have attachment issues. She's attached to the baby but she's known him from when he was born. So maybe for the second time in her life she has an attachment to someone. We have asked to foster her long term. We can't adopt her. Her birth parents are still alive and she meets them regularly.

RYAN: Amber's mum didn't stand a chance herself in life. We get on well with her. We tell Amber when she is a big girl she and her mummy will be friends. We say that to her mum too and she is getting the hang of the idea. It is only 11 years until Amber is 16 and then she can make her own mind up. Fostering Amber is like a job but our hearts are really in it.

RACHEL: Amber is a pretty girl and her looks and her brains might be just enough to take her where she needs to go. But it is difficult. She has huge issues. Both socially and emotionally she is very young compared to her academic level. She is a very bright girl, but in common sense and day-to-day care of herself she isn't so good. She is not very trusting; she only trusts herself. It's survival of the fittest and that's that. She has had to bank on just herself for too long. We can only change her environment but we hope for the best. What we love most about Amber is her enthusiasm for learning new things. We are doing our best to help Amber and we are trying to make her part of our family. It is both challenging and rewarding, but we are committed to helping this little girl.

Rachel, 37; Ryan, 39

Helping to create a community spirit

I am of the opinion that my life belongs to the whole community and as long as I live, it is my privilege to do for it whatever I can.

George Bernard Shaw

Bursting with energetic enthusiasm, Sally talks about her job as a community co-ordinator and how she aims to make her neighbourhood a better place for people to live in.

We have a community centre and we use this as the base for things like school holiday programmes and community group meetings. Apart from that I support other community organisations. I help with funding applications and I do administration work for groups. We have a lot of equipment that different groups can borrow. Sometimes if an organisation is struggling I go and work on their committee for a while and help get them back on track. My job description is probably summed up by saying that I'm helping to make the community a better place to live.

We provide a lot of activities for families that don't cost anything and we try and find activities for all age groups. We have a huge summer programme and do about 50 events each year. We take a vanload of play equipment around the beaches and reserves in the weekends and after school during summer. We have a garden party every year for the oldies. They absolutely love it: they get dressed up in their hats and we have cucumber sandwiches. We do a book fair every year. Kids bring along second-hand books, games and CDs and sell them. We had a storyteller come along this year and we had some free workshops for the kids. It's great! The kids can sell their books and make a bit of money, and they can then spend some money on new books from other kids. I also work with the local churches. We have two carol services each year and I also organise the Christmas parade.

We come up with new ideas every year. We respond to things in the community and we get people suggesting ideas to us. We had a mum say to us that it would be good to run a baby-sitting course for teenage girls. So we tried it and we had such a huge response we have done these courses now for eight years. We have had over 500 kids through this baby-sitting course. We teach them first aid, CPR, child safety and things like that.

One of my favourite events is the teddy bears' picnic. That was the first event I ever did so it is special. It is so rewarding. I have a class of intermediate kids that come and help out. We send invitations to all of the pre-schools and new-entrant classes and we get about 500 kids down there on the village green. We have a train, musical entertainment, face-painting and things like that.

I am also a Justice of the Peace. The other day I had a person come in who urgently needed a document signed. I was out there at the teddy bears' picnic but the staff let me know this was urgent so I went to meet this person. I had bare muddy feet, some kid had painted a star on my face and I had glitter in my hair. The person needing a document signed thought it was hilarious. So it can be amusing juggling the two roles!

Part of my job is letting people know about the hundreds of organisations that work in the community. People will often come to me with a bright idea of something they would like to do. I can say to them, 'You should talk to so-and-so because that is the sort of thing that she is doing. Maybe you can help her rather than setting up on your own.' People have great ideas but they often don't know what else is going on.

If people want to volunteer in the community, I would pin them down on what they want to do. You need to find out if they like working with little children, old people or teenagers. Are they arty? Are they sporty? Volunteer work is just as important as applying for a paid job. You have to find something to match their skills.

We get a lot of new immigrants that can't get work and they often do voluntary work. We have a lot to do with new immigrants. We started up an International Friendship Group 10 years ago. That meets every week. Half the people are Kiwi, the other half immigrants. They practise their English and we talk about New Zealand. It helps them understand Kiwi customs. For example, there was a Korean woman who received a letter from school asking her to go along to a parent evening and she was absolutely terrified. In Korea you only ever go to school if your child is in trouble. We had to explain to her about the link between school and home in New Zealand and how it is a different approach to schools in Korea.

Everything in my job is about community. I type the word 'community' on my computer so often that now I have it so I just press another key and 'C' and up comes the word 'community'! Community is the word that drives everything. My approach is that we can help people by feeding their spirit. We get people out in the community having fun, meeting their neighbours and building relationships. I've been doing this job since 1991 and it's not like a real job. If I didn't have to earn a living I would do it voluntarily. My job is so cool because it's so positive and it's all fun stuff.

Sally, 40s

Helping children with cancer

Sometimes to relieve,
sometimes to heal,
always to console.

The philosophy of Nurse Maude, the pioneer of district nursing in New Zealand

The Child Cancer Foundation has been helping children with cancer for more than 25 years. Parents and the medical profession have banded together to provide practical and emotional support for the families who have a child with cancer. And their work has made a huge difference: 25 years ago most children who had cancer died; today there is a 75–80% survival rate.

I've seen another dimension to life with kids with cancer that supersedes all the hustle and bustle of life. We had an experience with Carl that probably changed our lives as a family. He was only with us for a short time, but he certainly gave us a lot in this short time. I am very privileged to have had the opportunity to be involved in the Child Cancer Foundation. I've seen the power of support. I've seen miracles happen with kids. I've built friendships that are really enduring. The Child Cancer Foundation is not about structures. It is about sharing and caring. I'm very privileged to have been able to share and care with a lot of other people.

Paul, former Chairman of the Child Cancer Foundation

My role has been to be a friend to these children. I am hopefully someone they can trust. And often children can't ask their parents everything as they are too close to them, so they ask me instead.

Janette, Child Cancer Foundation volunteer for more than 25 years

I was in the timber business and we used to put piles of scrap wood out on the road and ask for donations for the Child Cancer Foundation. It worked really well. We supported child cancer for 10 years to the tune of thousands of dollars.

Jim, whose son Martin died two days short of his eighth birthday

I was invited to go to the first meeting of the Child Cancer Foundation 25 years ago and I've been part of it ever since. They kindly asked me to be patron. Children with cancer are close to my heart. It started off as such a small organisation in Auckland and now it has grown to be a national organisation. It's an extraordinary success story.

Two things that are quite outstanding are the character of the children. They have got something really special. And their families are very special too. They have to change their lives when they have a really sick child, and adjust to many things, and this is where I think the Child Cancer Foundation helps them so much.

I think the success that has been achieved with the children is absolutely fantastic. The medical profession are the most dedicated group of people ever. They are always prepared to do more. In fact, everyone involved with the foundation is prepared to do more – which in this day and age is very wonderful.

Lady Blundell, Patron of the Child Cancer Foundation

When you have a child diagnosed with cancer, it hasn't changed if it was 50 years ago or five months ago. The emotions and the feelings are still the same. To know there is assistance is important. That's why I was happy for parents to phone me. I'd get phone calls at 11 at night, at 1 a.m. – but that's the time parents are feeling at their lowest and that's when they want to talk to somebody. And the social workers don't work then, so that's where the job was satisfying because you knew that you could help those people.

Sue, volunteer for Child Cancer Foundation for more than 18 years, mother of a child who died and grandmother of a survivor

What we are seeing now is a very substantial number of cured children. Most of these people have some late effect or legacy of their experience. The role of the Child Cancer Foundation now is to ensure that the effects from childhood cancer don't limit that person's opportunity in life. These issues are medical and emotional and practical: things like jobs and insurance.

There is a common bond with everyone in the Child Cancer Foundation. Everyone has suffered in one way or another. We have survivors of life. We have had the experience of going through something and coming out the other side and then seeing the world through different eyes.

David, paediatric oncologist

A listening ear for people in need

What do we live for if not to make life less difficult for each other?

George Eliot

Articulate and caring, Ben talks about the volunteer work he has done for Youthline for the past three years.

I'm an accredited phone counsellor, which means that I have done a certain number of hours before I was allowed to go solo on the phone. To be a phone counsellor you have to do some training. First off you have to do a personal development course, which is 10 sessions that are two-and-a-half hours each. You do this to find out if you have any trigger issues. It also gets you in an environment where you can open up as well. I found that hard to do. I didn't understand it then but I think now it is important to be able to do that. It also helps knowing that there is support there. If you get something you can't handle there are people you can talk to about it.

I probably do 6-10 hours a week. It varies from week to week. You are contracted to do at least two shifts a month if you are a phone counsellor and each shift is three hours long. This semester I'm also leading groups. At the moment the group that I'm leading is almost ready to go on the phones by themselves.

I'm a university student and I have a part-time job. I volunteered for Youthline because it is something that I have wanted to do for ages. When I moved up to Auckland I gave them a call. I thought it was something I might do for half a year but it has been a really good experience and I've now been volunteering there for three years. It's good at giving you counselling experience. It's something I'm thinking about for the future. I don't know. I haven't made up my mind what I want to do in life.

I'm motivated to help other people, but I'm also motivated to do something for myself. I feel very good at the end of a session. I feel I've done something for the community. Youthline is quite community orientated.

Most of the people I have flatted with have ended up involved in Youthline. And I've met a lot of people at Youthline. Instead of going out and catching up for coffee we will go in and do a shift together. Last year we had a marae trip and I met heaps of people there.

We get all sorts of calls. Generally we are a support line, rather than a counselling line that gives advice. We reflect back what we hear and we provide a place where people can open up and talk. Any suggestions we usually come to together. I might say, have you thought of such and such? We will explore these different options. You go through the different scenarios – if they do this or that and what is likely to happen next.

There is no typical call. It's different each shift. The calls can be everything from rape, child abuse and drug problems to calls where people simply want someone to talk to. A lot of the older callers talk about things that happened to them a while ago. We have quite a big list of referral services for anything we can't handle, but mostly people just want to talk through an issue and we are able to make some suggestions.

I have noticed that if there is something good on TV the phone doesn't tend to ring. And it is also affected by the weather as well. Last Sunday it was raining heavily outside and in two hours I had taken 11 calls which is quite a lot when the average call is usually 20–30 minutes.

A few times it has been a bit distressing because I didn't know what happened: someone was screaming on the line and then the line went dead. With people's permission we would get the police or someone else involved if needed. Like if it is an overdose, we would say, is it all right to call an ambulance around to your house? A couple of times I've felt I've really made a difference. I had a call back once from someone saying thanks. That was really great.

I definitely believe people can make a difference in the community. They just need to find something that is right for them. I think if people don't like volunteer work it is because they haven't found something they enjoy doing yet. You have to choose something you enjoy so you will get something out of it as well as giving to others.

Ben, 20

City mission

The only cure for loneliness, despair and hopelessness is love.

Mother Teresa

Thousands of New Zealanders of all ages who are sick, disabled, lonely, in trouble or financially or spiritually deprived receive help from the city missions. The caring people in these missions assist people to help themselves. They help people to make positive changes in their lives and move on to a better quality of life.

I was studying a couple of years ago when I had a car accident. I was able to finish my studies at the end of the year, but I couldn't get a student allowance because the course was officially over. I had a part-time job, but couldn't get more hours. It was an awful situation. I was desperate. I ended up getting help from the city mission. They gave me some emergency food parcels. I don't know what I would have done without their help. I completed my studies and I now have a really great job. They helped me get my life back on track.

Emma, 24

I have worked for the city mission for the past 10 years. I used to look after the volunteers. There are so many people who do so many wonderful things. I also organised the Christmas dinner for seven years. A lot of the clients have very little during the year and the Christmas dinner is a major event in their lives and a very important one. So we always make sure that it is special. We hire a big marquee that seats 600 people and we have a band and entertainers. We also have a children's party. People have a lovely sit-down dinner. We have 100 volunteers who put the dinner together and serve the dinner. We have everything colour co-ordinated with red, green and gold.

One year we were short of soft drink. A guy rang up wanting to donate and asked us what we needed for Christmas. People are wonderful. I said we needed soft drink for the tables and that we would like red, green and yellow please. He said, 'No sweat!' The boxes arrived and we put them on the table so there was this whole theme running through it.

The city mission has a variety of social services. There is a drug and alcohol detox; an emergency shelter; a drop-in for families; a budget service; and a food bank. I'm now the operations manager. I look after the buildings, the maintenance, the vehicles, any operational part. I love my work. It is not one of those do-gooder things, but we do make a lot of difference in the community. It is a team effort. It can be a very sad sometimes to see what happens to people and why they are that way. Some people live with a great deal of adversity yet they can still smile. I don't know how some people get through a day, but they do. Some of them live on the street, yet they are so cheery and bright. People have such a strong spirit.

Paula, 50s

Saving the world

But while we're waiting
We could try saving the world
Or are we storing that up for a rainy day?

Brooke Fraser

Maureen did her nursing training with the intention of working in third-world countries. She shares some of her experiences of working in Africa.

The start of my interest in third-world countries came about because I had an aunt and an uncle that were both missionaries. I learnt very early on that there were people a lot worse off than us in the world. I always wanted to travel – but I wanted to travel with meaning. I met my husband, Ian, at a party and he was on a similar quest.

We got placed in Lesotho, a small independent country in southern Africa. Ian worked on rural development and I did the nursing. Lesotho is a beautiful place but a sad community of people. A lot of men go off to the mines and live a single-man's lifestyle and come back to their villages with VD and alcohol problems.

We lived in Lesotho for two-and-a-half years and our first son was born there. My husband worked on putting pumps and bore holes in place that brought clean water to villages in the area. Then Ian was made the engineer for the southern half of the country, bringing gravity-fed water supplies into the villages. It was a large area and very mountainous. He used to ride on horses to some of the villages as that was the only access.

I put a proposal forward and got some money from Oxfam. We set up a village health-worker training programme. I was able to employ a local nurse and a local woman who knew the area and knew how to talk to the chiefs. It would usually take half a day to walk to a village and half a day to walk back.

The courses were wonderful. Unlike English-speaking countries, the people are a lot more open and they are very into drama and singing. So we would act out the scenarios, like what do you do when your husband comes home drunk, that sort of thing. Then we got to know someone who was bringing Canadian money into the country. He gave us money and we built a primary health-care clinic. We managed to get a nurse to work full time and we also ran courses there.

I have always believed that whatever happens shouldn't be from the top down but instead from the bottom up. So often in underdeveloped countries you get the big brass coming in: they've got the money, they've got the power, but they don't actually know what the people want. When we were in Lesotho, we saw many projects that failed because they didn't consult enough with the people.

My husband set up a chicken co-operative. He sat around under the trees talking to people about how co-ops work, and how the co-operative would only work if they grouped together to buy and sell grain and chickens. Every person had to build their own chicken coop. Ian designed the chicken coops himself to try and avoid rats. He used only local materials. It worked really well because people had ownership of it.

We set up a sewing co-operative where people could make school uniforms and things. When I was trying to set up the sewing co-operative I was aware that a few nuns were getting crate-loads of clothing. They would sell the clothes to the people at high cost, but the prices were low enough to undercut the local tailors and dress-makers. It was not a good situation. People need to be careful about the organisations they give to because some organisations don't help the local people – they actually exploit the situation. Oxfam would be my number-one charity to give to. They do things from the bottom up and they do a lot of consulting with the people. But there are a number of other good charities also.

After we finished in Lesotho we had a contract to go to Mozambique. There was a civil war going on for all the time we were there, with appallingly cruel things happening. My husband helped to rebuild the sewerage system in the city of Beira. I worked in the mother and child clinics around the city trying to get them to function. It was very difficult work. People at the time were so busy trying to get food onto their own tables they didn't have a lot of energy left for anything else.

I think we especially made a difference in Lesotho. We went back two-and-a-half years later and the chicken co-op had actually mushroomed. They had built another building and they were raising little chicks and they were selling them to other places. And the sewing co-op was still going. This is unusual.

In Mozambique we made a difference in that when we left the sewerage system was much improved. In my area of nursing, it was hard to make a difference because the war was going on. There were a huge number of refugees that poured into the city. Life was very short. I would meet women who had had six children but had no live child. Death was very commonplace. In one particular area that was very low lying, when it rained it would flood up to your knees and people would try to sleep on tables. You would hear stories of children falling off tables in the middle of the night and drowning because no-one had noticed. TB was rampant. Aids was rampant. I had a man working for me who got news that his wife was sick. At 2 p.m. he went home and his wife was dead by 5 o'clock. She had had diarrhoea and vomiting for one day – but she had no resilience; no strength to fight back.

Working in third-world countries has definitely changed my outlook on life. If I meet another person with a different accent I want to welcome them and know all about them. I think it is sad that we don't know how well off we are. Even I forget how well off we are. We don't know the extent of other people's suffering. Even though it is seen on TV, I don't think it brings it home to us. The world is so wealthy yet we have vast areas where people are in misery. To have this situation in the 21st century shows something is radically wrong.

There is a lot we can do to help people, however. The most important thing to me is that we learn to be tolerant. The world is very small now and we have difference all around us. We can't get away from it. So people shouldn't say they want New Zealand to be the way it was, because they are never going to get that. Things are going to change. Life is all about change.

Maureen, 50s

Epilogue

Love is the subtlest force in the world.

Mahatma Gandhi

Do you ever feel you don't have enough love in your life? Do you feel like your family doesn't understand you? That you don't have any close friends? That you would like a life partner, but you are unconfident about opening up to another person? This is in your power to change. The first step is to believe in love. Believe also that you are worthy to be loved. Trust that you can love and be loved back. And have faith that love can last. With this in mind, go out into the world and be ready to love.

Make new friends; nurture your old friends. Treat your family members with care and compassion. Do something kind for another person less fortunate than yourself. Allow yourself to be open to the possibility of an intimate relationship. Don't be afraid to love. The benefits outweigh the risks of rejection or loss. Love is supremely important. It is the benchmark that we measure our lives against. Success in life is not about money or possessions, power or prestige; it is about living a full life and loving well.

Love is not a beautiful garden of flawless roses. There will be challenges that will impact on your relationships with others. There could be the death of a loved one, addiction, betrayal, money troubles, depression or health issues. There are any number of difficult things that can happen in life. But with patience, flexibility, forgiveness and understanding, love can not only survive these traumas but also flourish. Love is neither dumb nor blind. It sees the pain, can remember the wound, but is willing to work through it to start over again. That is the mystery and power of a love that is true.

With every gesture, word and action you are delicately sculpting your relationships. So choose your gestures wisely, be kind with your words and be thoughtful with your actions. Love is something that you do because you have made a commitment to love; the feelings follow from the action. And sometimes you just need to shine a light on things to make you aware of love. Don't shine a light on whatever might be wrong. You will only feel sad. Shine a light on all that is good and you will glow. Don't opt for cool reserve.

Look around. Is that your wife waiting to greet you with open arms and a loving kiss — even though you were grumpy to her when you spoke to her last? Is that your friend on the phone inviting you around for dinner simply because they want to spend time with you? Is that your mum washing your rugby clothes without complaining about the mud because she knows you enjoy the game? Is that a complete stranger who has just pulled over and helped you change a tyre on your car, simply because you needed some help?

Love, alofa, aroha is all around: just open your heart to it.

Gratitude

A huge thank-you to the wonderful Helen Benton and Bob Ross for their support and encouragement. Thank you to the team at Random House – and in particular Tom Beran, Jenny Hellen, editors Judith McKinnon and Claire Gummer and designer Christine Hansen – for their expertise and care.

Thank you to the many, many people who feature in this book. You are too numerous to list, but thank you for your warmth and wonderful generosity in answering my numerous questions about love. You are all special, inspirational people and it has been a privilege to hear your stories of love. Writing this book is a blessing I will cherish always.

Quotation credits

Something so strong, could carry us away . . . (page 28)
Used with permission of Neil Finn and Mushroom Music Publishing.

The great love I have hitherto expressed to you . . . (page 32)
From Amelia Webb letter to Nicholas Loye, in *Posted Love: New Zealand Love Letters*, ed. Sophie Jerram, published by Penguin Books. Used with permission of Alan Loye.

Oh, my love, my love . . . (page 36)
From 'At Last'. Used with permission of Iain Sharp.

We total 2 That's quite okay . . . (page 39)
From 'Two of Us', *Ecstasy*, published by Bumper Books. Used with permission of the estate of Alan Brunton.

Always, there are our hearts to consider. (page 44)
From 'Weighing up the Heart', *Miss New Zealand – Selected Poems*, published by Victoria University Press. Used with permission of Jenny Bornholdt.

In love, what do we love . . . (page 47)
From 'In Your Presence'. Used with permission of the estate of Charles Brasch.

Lovelier are her words . . . (page 56)
From 'When She Speaks'. Used with permission of the estate of A.R.D. Fairburn.

Drowning is easy, my darling . . . (page 58)
From 'Bon Voyage'. Used with permission of Alistair Te Ariki Campbell.

I can't get past the way I feel for you . . . (page 64)
From 'Still in Love'. Used with permission of Brooke Fraser.

It is the absurdity of family life . . . (page 68)
Quotation from *M.I.L.K. Family*. Used with permission of James McBride and PQ Publishing.

Lay your head upon my shoulder . . . (page 78)
From 'Close Your Eyes'. Used with permission of David Feehan.

I am bright with the wonder of you . . . (page 81)
From 'Brightness'. Used with permission of the Denis Glover estate and Pia Glover.

I like animals because they're honest . . . (page 94)
Used with permission of Bob Kerridge.

We can do what we wanna . . . (page 140)
From 'Waste Another Day'. Used with permission of Brooke Fraser.

Something that rises . . . (page 152)
From 'Ariel', *Cargo*, published by Voice Press. Used with permission of Bob Orr.

But while we're waiting . . . (page 180)
From 'Saving the World'. Used with permission of Brooke Fraser.

Every effort has been made to trace copyright holders. The publisher would be pleased to hear from any not acknowledged here.

Photography credit

Thanks to Devonport Garden Centre for allowing Christine Hansen to photograph its native plants.